[illegible] love for another [illegible] multidimensional soul. Enjoy! Jan Lemuri

Inner Dolphin Awakening

Opening Time Capsules of Joy, Telepathy and Multidimensionality

Jan Lemuri

Self-published

TAOS, NEW MEXICO

Copyright © 2018 by **Jan Lemuri**

All rights reserved. No part of this publication may be reproduced, distributed or transmitted in any form or by any means, without prior written permission.

www.innerdolphinawakening.com

Cover Design by Deborah Delisi

Editing by Rebecca Blue Rossi

Proofreading by Chelsea & Chloe

Book Layout © 2018 BookDesignTemplates.com

Inner Dolphin Awakening/ Jan Lemuri. -- 1st ed.

ISBN-13: 978-1720596851
ISBN-10: 1720596859

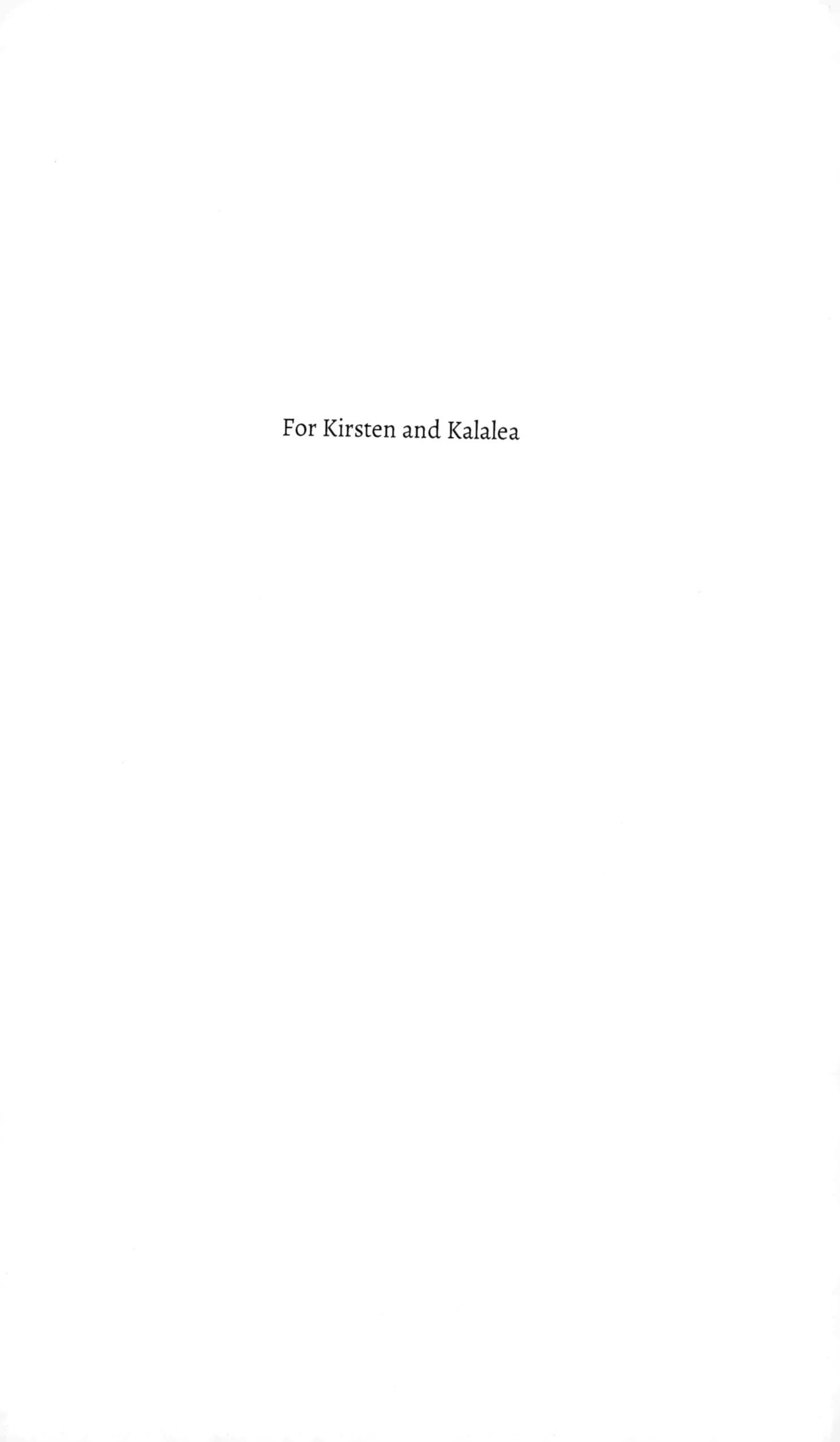

For Kirsten and Kalalea

Contents

• INTRODUCTION •

Transformation

HAVE YOU EVER READ A BOOK and when someone asked you what it was about your answer came in one simple sentence? Have you ever wondered why masters just smile instead of saying anything at all? The experience of inner knowing cannot be replaced by words. It cannot be explained, the only way to grasp it is to take the journey yourself.

This book is not trying to explain the unexplainable. It is an invitation. If there was one sentence, that would describe the whole book it would be, "What if everything you knew to be true about dolphins was inside you?" But maybe it would be better to just smile. Like the masters do. And extend a hand of invitation. Are you ready to take my hand and embark on a journey with me?

I was standing in a murky kitchen of an old Venetian building in a little coastal town of Croatia. Outside I could hear the voices of evening crowds strolling along the ocean promenade searching for a perfect place to sit down and enjoy dinner. There was that unique Mediterranean smell in the air, where the flavors of freshly grilled fish, garlic, and olive oil mix with the stale smell of fishing boats and the sea.

There was a single light on in the kitchen, and although the house was a family place with lots of coming and going, I found myself alone with a mysterious woman, Marinella, that I'd just met a few hours earlier. We were standing in the middle of the kitchen, just looking into each other's eyes. She was a beautiful, smiling, goddess-like older woman and was the reason I came to this town.

"She is like a mermaid. Her husband is a fisherman and sometimes, while out on the ocean, dolphins come to play at their boat." were the words of my friend who had told me I had to go and meet her.

So here I was, hoping that in the next day or two, I would be taken out on a boat and have yet another magical experience with dolphins, maybe even swim with them, who knows. But instead of chatting with Marinella about that, I was lost in her gaze. Her presence was enchanting, in a good way. I felt completely safe and any thoughts of past or future disappeared.

We hugged, and I could feel her fingers run alongside my back, gently following invisible energy pathways – an ancient Peruvian practice I would later learn she was adept in. I've experienced many different energy and bodywork modalities in my life, but what happened next took me by a total surprise. I started to feel and observe my body shifting, I was morphing, changing form!

My awareness first centered on my nose as I felt it grow longer; change color and texture. It morphed into a dolphin nose.

The experience continued with my mouth, which transformed into a dolphin smile. And then my eyes, which were now looking out with that gentle, loving dolphin gaze. As the skin on my head changed I could feel a blowhole open where the crown chakra is. I took a deep breath as my body shifted and transformed even further.

My hands repositioned themselves, my elbows pressed into the sides of my body and my arms opened outwards. They became pectoral fins. At the same time, I felt my heart open with a burst.

I followed the process down my spine and arriving at my tailbone saw a beautiful dorsal fin grow out from my body. The thought that went through my mind in that moment was, "Oh, my God, they didn't tell us the truth in school. We hadn't had a tail there, we'd had a dorsal fin!"

And then, as this strange process reached my knees, everything stopped. I was standing there in the middle of the kitchen, a dolphin on two legs. I was looking at my feet wondering if that's how it's supposed to be. "Am I to walk on land in a dolphin body? Am I keeping my feet so I can ground my energy into the Earth? Actually, how do dolphins connect with Gaia?"

The answer came in the form of a vision. I saw a dolphin's tail in its triangular shape and understood it's a symbol of how dolphins are connected to mother Earth. They are not just connected. They are Gaia herself. From her infinite consciousness, the soul of the planet focuses her being into a single point, the body of a dolphin. Dolphins' tail stands as a symbol of this process: starting wide open (infinite nature), it comes together into a single point (individual nature). Gaia is literally embodied in every cetacean. They don't need to ground themselves. They ARE one with the soul of the planet.

As this understanding resonated through my whole being I could see the rest of my legs and my feet turn into a dolphin tail. The transformation was complete. I had become a dolphin.

• CHAPTER 1 •

Look Inside

A VERY CLOSE FRIEND OF MINE once asked me, giggling, "Your soul doesn't know geography all that well, does it?"

"Why is that?" I wondered.

"Because you were born so far away from the ocean!"

It is true. I was born in an Alpine valley in a little country called Slovenia. I would only see the ocean once a year for summer holidays and that was my favorite time of the year. Otherwise, my childhood was mostly spent around forests, hills, and rivers. So how did I end up being so intertwined with the ocean and dolphins?

I can't speak about dolphins if I don't speak about my spiritual awakening first. You will see throughout this book that my dolphin journey is interwoven with my journey of self-discovery, and they really are one and the same. This chapter therefore presents seeds of understanding, a broader picture that lays a foundation for comprehension of cetacean truths.

I was brought up as an atheist. My father was a geologist and would explain the world and every phenomenon around us through the lens of science. His understanding was that nothing existed beyond what can be experienced with the 5 senses. Even emotions were perceived as weak and needed to be controlled rather than expressed.

My mom on the other hand was a nurse, where feeling was more important than thinking. But still talking about anything outside of the tangible, physical world didn't really exist in our family. That was in part because religion was seen as something evil and misleading – so anything that involved spirit, soul, energy healing and belief was never discussed.

That means I was growing up in a box of limited thinking without even knowing it, or as I would call it, the bubble of mind. It was comfortable, because mind sees life as a mathematical equation; it loves to play with predicting, evaluating, and controlling. It was also lonely, because the world of the mind locks out the qualities of the heart: compassion, intuition, excitement, and the ability to dream.

Opening My Heart

I was 16 when my bubble suddenly burst. As far as I remember, I was always in love with traveling. My family would do a lot of exploring within my own country, but I had a deep desire to go beyond. One sunny afternoon, while playing basketball with a classmate after school, he asked me if I wanted to go to Taize.

"What is that?" I wondered.

"It's a community in central France. Every summer thousands of people come there, young people, like you and me. They come from all over Europe, Africa, the Americas, everywhere. It's so much fun and most importantly, there's all these girls!" said my friend with a sparkle in his eye.

"I'm in!" I announced without hesitation. I could feel the excitement build within me.

"Ahem, there's only one thing. It's a community of Christian brothers that welcomes everybody. There's prayer three times a day."

"What?!" My spirit began to sink. How in the world would I, an atheist, suffer through so much prayer?

My friend had a solution. "You don't have to attend the prayers if you don't want to, so don't worry about it. Just come with us, we're going to have a blast!"

And we did. In my teenage mind, it didn't take long to put all the pros and cons together and realize that thousands of girls from places like Sweden, Spain and Brazil outweigh the discomfort of pretending I know anything about the Bible or prayer.

I was busy spending my days in Taize trying to come up with the best pick-up line while sitting outside the church, waiting for prayers to finish, so I could see all the girls come out from a perfect angle. In fact, I was so busy I never noticed something else was happening inside me. I only realized it when I got home. While I did end up having a one-night romance with a girl from Austria (who never ever answered my love letters afterwards), Taize gently touched and awakened parts of me I didn't even know existed.

Being back home I felt something was different, like there was a new depth to my feeling, but I had no words to describe it. Now looking back, with all simplicity, I can say this: My heart opened. My comfortable mind bubble burst, and in started to flow the knowing from my Akash; suddenly, I started to wonder why we were here, what happened after death and if there was some kind of a higher power.

And then I got sick. Really sick, bed-ridden for a week. My parents took me to see a doctor; I got antibiotics that seemingly worked for a few days only for me to get extremely sick again a week later. This repeated, on and off, for eight weeks. In the process, I was so bored I picked up random books and started reading them. One of them really got my attention because it was so different. It spoke of elemental beings and nature spirits. The subject was so foreign to me it had me struggling, trying to grasp any kind of understanding. Until I turned a page and there it was, a message (it seemed) just for me, "Illness is trying to tell you something."

What, how, why? I was flabbergasted. Isn't an illness just an illness? What is it trying to tell me? And why does my illness keep coming back, week after week? Why does it look like this sentence was placed in this book just for me, waiting for this exact moment?

Instead of getting answers, these questions gave birth to more questions. I became knowledge-thirsty, I went to the library and borrowed piles of books on spirituality, religion and occult sciences. I started to read, anything and everything. Whoever has the answers, I want to know, please! My disease, that no doctor had been able to define or explain, seemed happy with my approach, because it dissipated as I immersed myself in my studies.

At the same time, I found a local yoga group, where I could start experiencing some of the topics I was reading about: mediation, self-inquiry and awareness.

Throughout this process, I felt like a whole new world opened on the inside and outside and, strangely enough, I felt right at home. Soon I was starting to share my discoveries with people. More often than not I was misunderstood and rejected, so I quickly learned my first lesson. *Respect people and their beliefs. If you discover something exciting, it doesn't mean everybody has to believe it for it to be real.*

Healing with Universal Energy

Shortly after that, my world expanded yet again. I was walking home from school with a friend, who I thought looked amazingly cute and attractive wearing dreadlocks, rolling tobacco, and singing songs from Jim Morrison and The Doors all the time. I was explaining my newly-found interests in spirituality (trying to impress her and maybe even ask her out), when she looked at me and said, "Have you heard about Reiki?"

"No. What is that?"

"It is healing with universal energy. You get attuned to the energy that is everywhere. You allow it to flow through you into other people and often healings happen."

It made perfect sense. Instead of studying about a God that lives somewhere far off, I get to connect with universal energy and feel it flowing through me. In other words, I get to experience God right here, inside me. What a concept!

The results of our conversation were far grander than I could have imagined at the time. Instead of going on a date with my attractive friend, I ended up going to a Reiki teacher for my first attunement.

I need to stop the story here to say that I want you to be aware of the uniqueness of each of our journeys. What worked for me may not work for someone else and vice versa. Even though we all have our own compass to follow, I am sharing my experience, trusting it will resonate in a perfect way.

Reiki is an amazing gift. After months of reading and studying I finally got to experience, feel, play and connect with energies. It brought to life all the concepts I felt true in my heart and allowed me to share them with friends and loved ones – without saying a word.

It also introduced me to the concept of guides – entities that are around each one of us for the purpose of helping us on our spiritual path. They have different roles and among other things they can assist in healing. I had no idea at the time how big their role would be in my life, I just enjoyed knowing they are around and did my best to honor them while practicing Reiki.

Channeling

It was a few months later that I was presented with a new understanding of guides. I was introduced to the concept of channeling. What is channeling you might ask? In most simple terms, channeling is connecting with an energy that is seemingly bigger than you, to bring it forth into this reality. In other words, channeling is translating something from multidimensional reality into language that can be understood by a human audience. It is not done just by a selected few, we all experience it in our lives at one point or another. Have you ever felt a strong inspiration, gone into "the zone," and start creating something? Where everything just flows, seemingly without your conscious control, and the result was just marvelous? This is a form of channeling. Be it poetry, music, painting, dance or even new inventions, the way channeling works is the same and can be done by anyone. You bring forth an energy, inspiration, creation, that goes beyond what you think is possible. Many known artists, storytellers, actors, dancers, and musicians will describe this process in their own words, but there is a great deal of similarities in their descriptions. Which confirms the idea that channeling is innate and natural.

A form of channeling that I refer to often in this book comes from guides, angels, ascended masters, or even your own soul. This is how most of the holy scriptures on the planet were written – by inspired humans that connected to higher levels of consciousness, and channeled beautiful words and concepts.

A friend of mine brought a whole pile of printed channeled writings to me, saying he thought I might be interested. Fresh from Reiki and feeling my guides, I was indeed very curious and sat down with the first channeling, called "Cosmic lattice," by an entity named "Kryon,"[1] only to find my English was not good enough to understand what was being said. I put the pile into a corner and didn't touch it until a few months later when I decided to give it another try. This time I was just aimlessly flipping through the pages, reading titles and one caught my eye, "A wave of darkness" by "Tobias."[2] Tobias' language was far simpler than Kryon's and easy to comprehend. It went straight to my heart. After a few words, I was sobbing uncontrollably, not understanding why. All I knew was I felt amazing, thick love pressing on my shoulders, literally like somebody was hugging me from behind. What I felt went beyond anything I experienced before, beyond any kind of human love. How is that possible? How can words carry so much energy?

I now know it was not just the words, but me opening up to where the message was coming from. What would you say if I told you there's a legion of beings on the other side, that have the deepest love for us, but are not able to share it until we sit down and open our heart? And what if these beings are not really separate, but are a part of us, just like flower petals are all a part of the same flower?

Kryon explained this in a beautiful metaphor.[3] He said to imagine a vast ocean. How many water molecules is there in an ocean? Billions. Now imagine a glass bottle, half filled, floating in this vast ocean. Is the water in the glass part of the ocean? Yes. But the water molecules in the bottle might have a hard time connecting with the molecules on the other side of the glass. They might even think they are all alone, not even knowing an ocean exists.

The water in the glass represents all the souls that are going through Earth experience and the glass represents "the veil of forgetfulness," a system of duality that allows us to forget who we are as souled beings. Each water molecule represents a single soul, an individual entity, but looking from a higher perspective, we are all water, we are all the ocean! We are not separate and when you feel that love coming from the other side, you start to remember the vastness of the ocean, the love of the family.

After my first experience of channeling I would sit in this love every day, reading page by page, not even caring if I couldn't understand certain words (and funny enough, that is exactly why my English improved over time). The energy behind the words would always come through and make me cry. It was so beautiful.

The Message

While each channeler translates the messages in his/her own unique way and every entity has a certain energetic signature (special way of presenting things), there are key points where they all align. If you step back and take a fresh look, you can see the message that emerges and is common to everyone.

Here is my summary of this message into five points:

Empowerment. You are not a victim of your circumstances and you are not here by accident. You are empowered to co-create your life, take the hand of your Higher Self, listen to your intuition and find peace in any circumstances.

No Armageddon. Humanity is not destroying itself. We passed the decision point and, as a collective consciousness, we chose to stay and evolve. We voided all the prophecies saying there was going to be a mass destruction at the end of the last millennium. Instead, there is an awakening coming unlike any we've ever seen before, and humanity will shift into a new consciousness, that will create a more peaceful, compassionate planet.

New gifts, new techniques. New energy on the planet is bringing with it new ways, that are often more graceful than what we've known in the old days. Things that took years to heal might balance very quickly now (if you will allow it). Watch for new teachings, methods, and techniques as a direct response to our changing consciousness. We are not to remove ourselves from society and live in seclusion, meditating on a mountaintop anymore. We are to live a "normal" life empowered with the new tools. Our compassion has an ability to touch the lives of everyone we meet. While there are too many gifts to mention here (your intuition will guide you to the right ones for you), there is one that might be the single, most important gift of this new time, and that is the next point in this summary.

Dropping Karma. Karma worked well in the lower consciousness throughout our history, making sure we kept working on our lessons through mostly unpleasant interactions within our karmic group. The biggest gift for an awakening human in this new time is the ability to drop karma, to take full responsibility for our growth, and solve our life lessons. You drop your karma by simply asking for it and then... enjoy the ride!

You are never alone. The veil to the other side is only as thick as you believe it to be. With your intent, asking and (metaphorically) stretching your hand through the veil, you start opening to your soul family. There are many benevolent energies right next to you, just waiting to be of assistance. The love that your spiritual family has for you is the most beautiful, profound, home-like feeling that will touch your innermost essence and remind you of the bigger picture. That love is here for you every second of every day. You are never alone.

Look Inside

My search for the holy grail, my thirst for knowledge and wisdom continued for a few years, I went from book to book, religion to religion, technique to technique. And then a message started to emerge from everywhere, quiet at first, but louder and louder as time went on. I didn't want to pay attention. Then it came in a form that was undeniable, so strong and clear, I couldn't ignore it anymore.

One day I was sitting on the edge of my bed, simply letting my mind wander while looking out the window, not focusing on anything in particular. It was one of those "meditations", where you think about life without any real direction, time passing, thoughts coming and going.

And then without any warning, I found myself in a vision. It was almost like somebody took me out of my body and placed me in a dream, the only difference being that everything was crisp and clear.

In my vision, I was part of a crowd of people, grouped according to our nationality. We were standing in a half circle, surrounding a man on a little stage. He was short, with darker skin and dressed in an orange robe. His hair stretched out in a big afro that gave him the distinctive look that millions of people around the world hold so dear to their hearts. I recognized him instantly even though I had never read or studied anything about him. He was Sai Baba, an Indian mystic and guru, known for his manifestations and miracles.

I watched as Sai Baba slowly turned from group to group in our half circle, delivering messages in different languages to each one. I was the last person in that half circle and I was standing alone. After finishing with everybody else, Baba turned to me, looked deep into my eyes, and spoke two simple words, that reverberated through my whole being, "Look inside!"

He hardly finished saying it when I was back on my bed, back in my body, with a look of bewilderment on my face. What just happened? Where did I go? Did I fall asleep? Not possible, especially with the way I was fully awake before and after. I didn't know what to do with the whole incident, so I just brushed it off and continued with my life as if nothing happened.

So the Universe, having to work around my not wanting to hear the message, had to keep finding new ways to deliver it to me. Next summer I went back to Taize, the little village in France where my whole journey had started a couple of years before. I was a different person this time though, with my ears and eyes wide open to learn something new. I was surprised to find I now enjoyed the prayers. It was special to sit down in stillness with a few thousand young people and sing beautiful one-line chants, my favorite being, "A soul filled with love does not get tired nor tires others." I loved the prayers so much I started to stay longer, realizing after the official part was over, lots of people kept on singing into the night. I also noticed that a few of the community brothers stayed around, standing silently to the side, allowing for anyone to come speak to them.

There was also the oldest of them, brother Roger, who founded the community in the 1930s, thinking it would be around 20 brothers sharing a simple lifestyle in prayer (the Universe sure did have some laughs about that one, when thousands of young people started to show up a few years later). Now he was in his mid-eighties and having difficulty walking, so he sat on a chair that was moved to the middle of the building, after the evening prayer was over. Then, hundreds of people would line up to receive his blessing – a gentle placing of his hand on top of their forehead. I've seen a very similar thing with Indian gurus and found it interesting how certain practices crossed the lines of different religions, almost as if we innately remember which gestures hold sacredness.

Not being of Christian tradition, I felt fine just observing, until a few days later, after I'd had one of those "I have no idea what to do with my life" moments. I felt sad, lost and alone, trying to find any purpose and direction. As I was looking at all the people lining up to receive brother Roger's blessing, I decided to join them. Receiving a blessing was kind of a quick process. People would kneel in front of him, Roger would place his hand on them for a few moments and off they went.

It was soon my turn and I was taken aback when instead of blessing me, Roger started speaking to me – he hadn't done that with anyone else! He spoke in French, so I said something about not understanding. He then spoke in English but was too quiet to hear over all the singing. I asked him to repeat and brought my ear closer to his lips. He spoke slowly, with a deep, raspy voice, "The light is in your heart!" He then blessed me, and I went back to my spot, sat down and cried for 15 minutes. This simple message, spoken from the beautiful light of brother Roger, cut through all the darkness and emotion I was muddled in, my tears washing everything away. Just like Baba, Roger directed me inward, back to myself.

I wasn't completely ready to get their message, I wasn't yet done with my search. I guess it was just too much fun to put responsibility outwards. Besides that, there was still a few more shelves in the "New Age, Occult and Mysticism" section of the library for me to go through.

So, life presented me with the same message yet again, for the third time (have you noticed there's something about number 3 and how it gets your attention?). It was my dear Tobias this time, a channeled guide I mentioned a few pages ago. Being with Tobias was so heart-warming and I did my best to follow the exercises he would give us every month. And then came his latest book, called a "New Energy Bible." It was supposedly a bible for the new times, because, as you might have noticed, the other one is over two thousand years old. Maybe some updates were needed, some new information? I opened this new book and it was utterly and completely empty, over 200 pages of it, except for the first page where it was written, "You are God also."

I finally got it. Whatever I was searching for was not outside. It was not in the books, religions, and techniques. So, I might as well stop trying to get enlightened through studying about it and start to listen to what my intuition was telling me. It was time to connect with the sacredness within me. It was time to find my soul!

Exercise 1: Drop into Your Core

Here is a meditation that helps you remember the simplest thing. You, the real you, is still there when you completely let go.

And it is done by using the breath.

It is as simple as breathing in and as you breathe out, releasing everything. You do it step by step or in other words, whatever arises in the moment of exhale, you simply let go. You will notice thoughts come and go. Release them.

You will notice your surroundings are there, as an expectation of a fixed, solid reality, including sounds, colors, objects, and walls. Let them go.

Feel yourself simply falling inwards, letting go of any attachment you have to this world. You need to trust yourself, that even if you let everything go, something will be there for you.

It is called your essence, your core, your soul.

It is your inner-most sense of self.

Keep letting go. Your families, jobs, to-do lists.

Personalities, emotions, dramas.

Everything can leave with an exhale.

You are not holding on, you are simply relaxing into the sweetness of your breath.

Let go. Let go. Let go.

Drop into your core.

Drop into your core.

Drop into your core.

CHAPTER 2

The Dream

DO YOU BELIEVE THAT DREAMS can foretell the future? Have you ever received a message that completely changed the direction of your life? That's what happened to me. My journey that took me to swim with dolphins and whales all around the world, had me live in different countries, had me sail across South Pacific and now has me writing this book; this journey started with a simple dream.

I am on a boat with a group of people. We just hang out and enjoy the ocean. The water surface is flat with no sign of any activity. And then suddenly, in a moment of clarity, I point at a specific spot on the water, saying, "Dolphins!" Everybody looks, and dolphin fins pop out. They only emerge after

I announce their presence. How did I know they were coming? It was a moment of telepathy and clairvoyance.

I did not feel connected to dolphins and whales growing up. I thought they were smart and good looking but nothing beyond that. I had taken no special interest in them. They seemed to be just another animal species. Which is why I was kind of surprised when they started to show up in my dreams. Not only once. I would have the same dream, repeatedly.

You can imagine how that would get my attention. After a while, I started to wonder what was going on. Why did this dream keep on coming back? Then just to spice it all up, I had another dream that started repeating:

I am underwater playing with dolphins. One of them approaches me and invites me to grab its dorsal fin. I am holding tight as the dolphin starts swimming faster and faster. The speed of the water rushing by is almost hurting my eyes, but I never let go.

Australian Aboriginal people believe that the whole world was created in the Dreamtime, a different reality that preceded our known physical world, almost like a matrix of sorts, where energies played out to create patterns that set life into motion.

In a similar way, these recurring dreams initiated a change in my life. They created an interest, wonder, curiosity. They became a riddle I was trying to solve: Why were my dreams repeating? What did it mean? I did my best to decipher what the metaphorical significance of each dream was.

I concluded dolphins represented passion for life. I started to wonder what kind of adventure I was being led on if dolphins were popping up all around me. A desire was born within me, to go and swim with dolphins for real. Thus, my dreams created a dream of another kind, a dream for the future.

Browsing through different options I concluded the place to go would be Hawai'i. It seemed like the best place to meet with dolphins in the wild. But how does a student in a little European country, that hardly makes enough to get by, save for the cost of a plane ticket to the other side of the world?

I mean, I was hitch-hiking 20 miles to my university every day, just so I could save a few extra bucks for my leisure time... Flying to Hawai'i just didn't seem to be realistic. But if I'd learned one thing in life, it was to never give up on my dreams. They came to me for a reason and I knew it was not about if, but when, were they going to manifest. Was I ok letting go of the timing and allowing for the perfect synchronicity to present itself?

I was. It took 5 years. I shifted and changed in the process and became a different person – I now understand I had to transform myself for my dream to be able to manifest. You see, when dolphins started to come to me, they helped me understand I was not supposed to separate myself from life, pretending to be all spiritual. I was to dive in fully and embrace life and everything it offered.

Living Fully

I became an editor of a student newspaper, started to write poetry, dance 5Rhythms and got into my first long-term relationship. I was following my passions for the first time.

My biggest passion, traveling, was not left behind either. I found cheap plane tickets to Iceland and flew there for a month to backpack, hitch-hike and camp. It was a freezing, but mesmerizing, experience. I fell in love with the way the land felt there. Natural wonders were spectacular to witness, but even more fascinating, was an energetic quality of purity that I hadn't experienced in other places. It felt crystal clear, sharp, fresh. My thoughts and feelings reflected that. Suddenly, I could think with increased clarity and open up to inspiration with greater ease. Why would that be?

Kryon has shared on numerous occasions that planet Earth, or Gaia, is much more complex than we think. He talked about three different grids: Magnetic, Crystalline and Gaia grid. Our science is only aware of the Magnetic grid, but we have problems understanding its multidimensional properties and how it's related to human consciousness.[1] Kryon's recommendation was to go live where it is cold, meaning the further from the Equator the better. It doesn't mean you can't be balanced in other places, it just takes less work to stay connected closer to the poles.[2]

The second grid, called the Crystalline, is there to remember everything that ever happened on the planet. Have you ever been somewhere, where you felt heaviness, suffering and sadness, almost as if it was etched into the land itself? Did you go back and check the history of that place and what happened (like wars or famine)? That would explain it, wouldn't it? Or on the other hand, have you ever felt unexplainable joy, celebration, and love? Trust me, the land remembers. Hence the name Crystalline, meaning it holds and remembers information. And here comes something you maybe didn't expect: Dolphins and whales are a back-up for the Crystalline grid! Everything that happened is not just stored on the grid but also in dolphins and whales. They are a living library.[3] We will come back to that later in the book.

If you want to understand more about the grids, Monica Muranyi from Kryon team, wrote a beautiful book called The Gaia Effect, where she explained in detail each of the grids, what they mean and how they work with human consciousness.[4]

The knowledge of the grids certainly answered my question, "Why does Iceland feel so pure?" Geographically it is almost as far north as possible, which creates magnetics where it's easier to stay balanced. Historically, it has only known civilization for a few hundred years, with no wars or huge trauma. With the absence of history all you can feel is Gaia, the soul of the planet.

Aloha Hawai'i

It was at the end of 2008, around 5 years after my first dolphin dream, when Hawai'i came to visit me. I know it's a funny way to say that, since people usually go visit Hawai'i, but here's what happened. I was doing a simple meditation where you see your future in a form of multiple possible realities. You imagine bubbles around you that represent your potentials. They are just floating in empty space, some of them are closer, some further away. Each bubble holds a reality, complete unto itself, that is one of the potential futures for you. As you go through life, your energy changes and attracts different bubbles closer to you. You can play with this exercise, looking into random bubbles, starting with the nearest one.

As I peeked into a bubble that was right in front of my face, Hawai'i was there, waiting for me. Warm sun, beautiful, white-sand beaches, and lush, green mountains. The energy was embracing me and calling me and every cell of my being responded.

"What a nice meditation" I thought, when I was done. "I wish it were true." And I brushed it off.

But the spirit of aloha stayed with me. I started to listen to Hawaiian music and daydream a lot, as the winter in Slovenia got colder and colder. I wasn't making any plans, I was just riding the energy. A few weeks later I accompanied my girlfriend to a travel agency. She wanted to find a good deal on flights to New Zealand. As she was going through all the options with her agent, I was bored so I sat down at the next window, hearing myself say, "How much would a ticket to Hawai'i cost?" I was just curious.

"If you're fine being flexible, we can go as low as $900," said the agent in a few minutes.

My breath stopped. That was doable, I could get that money together! I took a day to think about it, but I knew already, I could feel it inside. I was going to Hawai'i!

According to many channelers, the Hawaiian Islands are the mountaintops of an ancient continent, Lemuria, that was one of the first civilizations this planet had ever seen. I had a strong intuition that I've had a Lemurian lifetime and I was eager to see what would happen.

I will never forget landing and stepping out of the airport for the first time. The sounds, the smells, the air, the land... everything embraced me. I could hear a gentle whisper in the air saying, "Welcome home, welcome home."

This energetic greeting continued for days. Every cell in my body danced as my feet walked the ground they hadn't touched for so many lifetimes. There was something about the green mountains that surrounded Manoa valley, where I was staying, I could just sit and cry looking at the green peaks. Other places made me stop in the middle of my trek as goosebumps flowed up and down my legs. I had to take a few deep breaths, just allowing, while smiling with gratitude. I remembered. I celebrated. I was home.

Then the main confirmation came in the form of a vision. As synchronicity had it, I arrived on a Sunday and first thing in the morning, I attended Honolulu Church of Light, home to Signature Cell Healing, a modality brought forth by Kahu Fred Sterling.[5]

Their Sunday service is called a healing service. At a certain point, everyone is invited to either give or receive a healing. While I was there, people who felt they needed healing could sit on one of the four chairs in front and just relax. Everyone else would then circle them and place their hands on them, intuitively.

I sat on one of the chairs and expressed my intention for healing: to release fear of being in my full power. As the healing started, everything shifted, and I couldn't feel the people anymore, instead the space surrounding me was filled with thick love pressing on me from every possible direction. It was so strong I was crying within seconds and a few moments later I found myself in a vision.

I stand on a white sandy beach surrounded with green mountains. It is strikingly similar to Hawai'i, but it feels like it's from another time and space. In front of me is a dark skinned Polynesian boy, around 6 years old. As I look into his big, brown eyes, our gazes lock and I lose myself in the depth of his being. And then I experience a profound realization: I am that boy and the boy is me! That recognition fills my whole being with the deepest love and I cry in remembrance of my Lemurian self. I merge with it in love, gratitude, healing. After thousands of years, I come back to myself. I am complete.

Lemuria

In the next few weeks, I enjoyed traveling from island to island, feeling into what Kryon channeled about them while on a cruise in 2006. Hawaiian Islands were pushed out by a lava bubble to create a small continent of Lemuria, that sank around 26,000 years ago. What made Lemuria unique was not having any contact with the outside world for thousands of years, keeping the knowledge and wisdom of the ancients pure.

Each island of Hawai'i still carries a very specific energy connected to different Lemurian temples and ceremonies performed there. All the islands are actually peaks of one huge mountain, the tallest mountain on the planet, that is now mostly submerged. The mountain was once so high there were glaciers on top and they reached all the way down to where the beaches are presently.[6]

The sacredness of everything we did in Lemuria etched itself onto the Crystalline grid, and can be felt as you swim, hike and explore the islands. Could this be why so many people are drawn to Hawai'i?

Here's a little summary of what Kryon said about each island and its energy[7]:

Oahu and Maui were places of celebration and ceremonies.

Molokai was a place of healing.

The Big Island (Hawai'i) is where the temples of rejuvenation were. Lemurians were able to live hundreds of years, because they found a way to set their cellular age back to a youthful state.

Kauai was considered to be the most sacred, Lemurian couples climbed up there to get married. Kryon called it the island of love and said it's not a coincidence it was the only island that has never experienced any war.

I had a week on each island. I'm not a big city person, so I was surprised when I fell in love with Oahu, which was meant to be more of a stopover. I felt goosebumps every time I looked at the mountains and experienced amazing synchronicities with people.

Flying to Molokai was coming home. Time stood still, and the island has a charm of forgotten paradise. Hitchhiking opened a door to meeting locals and I was invited to spend time at their homes, some of them on ancient, sacred lands, that spoke to the deepest levels of my being. I was sitting on a beach one day, closing my eyes with gratitude overflowing. With my inner eye, I saw ground underneath me open and I traveled to the heart of the island.

I met with the soul of the island, that was like a being, spirit, deva... It had its own character, its own unique energetic signature and was beaming an incredible love at me, that melted my whole being. No words, just ancient love. At the same time space above me opened and I met with my guides. They also loved me beyond measure and I was in state of pure bliss, loved from underneath and above, crying tears of joy.

From that moment on I understood that each island has a soul, its own unique energetic pattern and if you're lucky enough, you get to experience the love it holds. That's why my suggestion to people when they go to Hawai'i is, "Talk to the soul of the island, it resides deep down under the surface, waiting for you with pure love. Ask to be guided, ask for synchronicities on your path."

Maui came next and this may come as a shock to many – it was my least favorite island. I did have a nice time there and witnessed amazing natural beauty but haven't felt a connection as strong as on the other islands.

Kauai was the most mystical and spiritual, almost like interdimensional energies found ways to embody into a physical form there. I could feel it everywhere. I hiked to the remote valley of Kalalau via a 17 mile long path winding up and down the cliffs of Na Pali coast. The path was dangerous, sometimes one wrong step would mean sliding hundreds of feet to certain death.

But the scenery was breath-taking, beyond anything I've ever seen. Razor-edged peaks loomed above rugged, green cliffs, waterfalls spouting out of sheer walls, cascading towards the ocean, clouds birthing rainbows and whale spouts in the distance. Every corner I turned left me speechless. The natural beauty was truly spectacular and unparalleled. At one point, I was so filled with gratitude, I thought to myself, "I am so blessed I could just die!" And then I almost did.

On my 2-day hike out of the valley, clouds covered the mountains and it started to pour like it was the end of the world. Little, cute streams turned into roaring madness and I needed all my skills to get over them, jumping from rock to rock, holding onto the tress... I was successful until the last one, 2 miles before the end. The river was already knee deep when I was hiking into the valley but now it looked strong enough to swallow a moose. I was wet, hungry, and ready to be done so I carefully waded in. It was hard to keep my balance, trying to feel the bottom, searching for good solid steps. The water was soon up to my chest and rushing past me with immense force, almost knocking me over. They say it's usually not easy to hear the voice of your innate body intelligence, but in that moment, mine was loud and clear, "Step another step here and you can say goodbye to this human life." My body just knew that if I lost balance, the river would take me, and I would drown. Luckily, I chose to listen, turned around and got out safely.

"Now what?" I wondered, as I stood there, shaking. I was wet, cold and had no food left. Even though I don't believe it happens this way, sometimes it seems like God sends angels, when we most need them. Three guys appeared out of the bushes, each with a pair of hiking poles and a look of "I've dealt with similar stuff in the Himalayas" on their faces.

They approached the river systematically, wading in on different parts and poking ahead with their poles to find the shallowest part – it turned out to be some 20 yards upstream from where I was. I smelled success and walked over to them asking if they could help me cross as well.

They smiled and made a "human bridge." They stood a few feet apart from each other, in the middle of the rushing water, extended hands, so I could walk from one to the other, crossing the river safely. Dear God, if they were angels, thank you! If they were humans, biggest thanks to our higher selves, for coordinating and timing this event perfectly!

The last island to fly to was Hawai'i, the Big Island, where I knew I could swim with dolphins. Would I finally fulfill my dream?

Inexperienced Fool

There's a little fishing village called Miloli'i on the Big Island. If you drive to the end of it and walk next to the ocean you will find a gorgeous black sand beach, with coconut palm trees providing just enough shade to make it possible to stay there for a full day – which is exactly what you want to do because the bay is so pristine and beautiful.

I had no idea Miloli'i even existed until I stayed with a guy that lived down the road from it and when I mentioned dolphins, he said I might be lucky and find them there. So, there I was, early next morning, loaded with excitement and sun screen. Only four other people were there besides me, two very friendly Canadians, who were chit-chatting with me before I even got to sit down, and a French couple, who were snorkeling in the water.

As I was talking with the Canadians, I looked out across the bay and saw a grey fin glistening in the sun. "Dolphins!" I shouted, pointing towards the bay. I couldn't believe my eyes. The dream I'd been dreaming for years was suddenly real, dolphins were here! How special! But they were very far, and I wasn't sure I should swim all the way out. I didn't want to end up in a rip current. So, I kept talking to my new friends, explaining that what they were seeing out there, was exactly what I'd traveled thousands of miles for. I then I decided to go and swim half way into the bay and see what would happen. Maybe the dolphins would come say hi?

As I was swimming I noticed the visibility underwater was just stunning, with white sand at the bottom and occasional coral here and there. Now I need to admit something that would make an experienced dolphin swimmer shake his head in disapproval: I didn't have any snorkeling gear! No fins, no mask, no snorkel. Just me, my shorts, and the ocean. You would think that a person willing to travel to the other side of the world to swim with dolphins would at least take a minute to check how it's done properly, but no, not me. I was just happy to be there. As a young boy, I loved reading books about the wild West and they had a name there for people like me, a greenhorn!

I made it half way across the bay and waited. I was diving down, singing, chatting, and clicking, knowing dolphins could hear me... but nobody showed up for the party. I swam back and sat on the beach. The dorsal fins were still out there. I decided to give it another try, again with no success. I walked back to my towel and as I was sitting down a dolphin came all the way to the middle of the bay and jumped out, spinning in the air, as if to say, "Come on!"

I ran back in and started to swim towards where the dolphin did his acrobatics. I was joined by the French couple and we were determined to get closer to the dolphin pod. As we were swimming we could see the fins ahead of us and got very excited. A moment later the French guy cried out, "One swam underneath me, I saw it!" Now, that really got us going! We were in such a high state of anticipation, it was almost like a trance. We felt like we were nearly there. The fins kept on popping out in front of us and it seemed like we could almost touch them. Ah, the joy of being with dolphins! Swim, swim, swim!

If only we had a little bit of our rational mind left, we would have noticed that the pod was keeping their distance and slowly moving out to the open sea. But we were too busy trying to get to them. And then in one moment we realized the fins were gone. Dolphins hadn't shown up for a while. We stopped and waited, looking all around us. Nothing. The dolphins had simply disappeared.

My heart stopped when I turned around and saw how far we'd swam. People back on the beach looked tiny! We were a long way from the shore. I started to swim back and soon all kinds of fears popped in. If you've ever swam a good distance, you'll know that it takes time for objects far away to start changing their size. In my case, palm trees and people stayed tiny for good 5-10 minutes and that's when my mind began to panic. "Am I in a rip current? Or even worse, what if the current is as fast as my swimming speed and I'm actually staying in the same spot, not moving at all?" "How much strength do I have left?" "Will I make it?"

These fears and doubts resulted in a big drop in my energy level. Fear froze my muscles and made it difficult to stay focused. Tears were streaming down my face as my mind tried desperately to come up with some kind of solution, in case I actually was in a current.

I am forever grateful for what happened next: The Canadian guy whom I was talking to beforehand, walked to the edge of the water, focused on me, and started to imitate big, slow swimming strokes, all the while keeping his eyes locked with mine. The support I felt was amazing, suddenly new energy rushed into my muscles and I could feel his movement charging me up. But most importantly, it brought me out of fear and I started to believe I could make it back. My Canadian friend stayed with me, continuing with the movement, until I climbed out of the water 15 minutes later and hugged him, thanking him with all my heart.

I laid down on the sand and celebrated being alive. I learned an important lesson that day. I shouldn't allow my excitement to get the better of me and try to force a meeting with dolphins. They can swim 5 times faster than humans and if a meeting is to happen, it will happen on their terms. And that's when I heard a voice inside me, condensing my feelings into one simple sentence, "Dolphins will come when you're ready!"

Dreams fulfilled

My first "dolphin swim" made me realize I had a lot to learn about the ocean and swimming with dolphins. I was an experienced swimmer in my dreams, but when it came to this reality, I was just a beginner. I decided to pay for an organized dolphin swim, to be guided into a meeting by people who had done it many times. We would approach dolphins on a boat. Fins, masks, and snorkels would be provided. I knew deep down this was the perfect next step. I was ready!

At 8am next morning I was a part of a small circle of people, gathered around our captain performing a chant in Hawaiian, expressing gratitude, and requesting the presence of dolphins. A few minutes later we were gliding on the water, with amazing views of Mauna Kea and Hualalai, two of five volcanoes that poured their lava out to create the island of Hawai'i.

"The pod is up North," said the captain after listening to a scratchy and broken voice on a radio that only he could decipher. I could feel a wave of excitement wash over our group as the boat headed towards the dolphins. We were motoring for a good 30 minutes, watching black lava cliffs that intermittently gave way to beautiful white sand beaches. And then we saw them – the fins on the water. Not ten or twenty, there were more than a hundred!

Mask. Check! Snorkel. Check! Fins. Check! Alignment. Oh yes, alignment! What did I learn? Dolphins will come when I'm ready? Ok. No rushing, zealotry, or rapid swimming. Peace, trust, and safe, welcoming energy. Check!

"Spread out and swim in different directions." were the instructions from the captain. I wanted to stay in my energy and didn't watch where everyone else was going. I started swimming with peaceful, yet deliberate strokes all the while I was repeating in my mind, "Dolphins will come when I'm ready. Dolphins will come when I'm ready." I knew it didn't matter where I ended up, my alignment was the key. I looked in the direction the dolphins were supposed to come from and couldn't see anything. I stopped. And then a sound reached me, clicks and whistles traveled through the water and hit my eardrums like a greeting from afar.

I looked again and there they were, two dolphins were swimming towards me. They spun around each other and passed me by, clicking and chatting. I was mesmerized as I watched them disappear in the distance. This was my first time seeing dolphins underwater – I was exuberant! Thinking I was done, I turned around and I'm sure if I had been standing on land I would have fallen on my bum. The whole pod was coming towards me!

There were moms and babies, there were dolphins deep down and up on the surface, some of them were playing and doing underwater acrobatics, others were just gently swimming. They were passing me by, some right next to me, looking straight into my eyes. Moms even brought babies to look at me. I was in the middle of a hundred-strong dolphin pod!

The beauty of the moment was so intense I started to laugh and sing with sheer joy. I was so grateful. I was in bliss! I took a deep breath and... breathed in water! My pure ecstasy made me forget the basics of snorkeling, *"Always keep your snorkel out of the water!"* Dolphins, who until that moment wore loving, peaceful gazes, now had a wondering look on their faces, they seemed to be saying, "Hey human, are you ok? Do you need a back pat?"

I couldn't believe it, I was coughing uncontrollably trying to get all the water out of my lungs, while the whole pod of dolphins was swimming past me. How did I get so lucky?

All was not lost though, we had a chance to go in the water a few times that day. The pod would swim past us, we would get back on the boat, pass them in a half circle and meet them in the next bay. The best news was that my approach worked! I was repeating the same sentence whenever I left the boat, swimming away from everybody else and was blessed with the whole pod every single time!

There was one more surprise that day. Waiting for the dolphins in one of the bays we heard a loud spout and then another one. It was a mama whale with her baby! We turned the engine off to see what they would do. They approached our boat and baby swam underneath us, playfully turning and showing us his belly. Such a precious encounter! What a gift!

When the tour was over, I felt a fulfillment like never before. There's nothing like dreaming a dream for years and having it come true. If I can be a bit poetic, I felt like I was a fountain of love, bubbling with joy and overflowing with bliss. As I was sharing all this with a friend, saying my dream was finally fulfilled and my mission was complete, I heard a voice inside me say, "Yes... And I want to do it again. And again. And again."

Exercise 2: Understanding Synchronicity

Have you ever heard that things happen in their own perfect timing? What does that mean? Is it possible that the Universe is trying to support your dreams?

When you understand how synchronicity works, you can start relaxing with the flow of life. Synchronicity is a benevolent event, that brings about what you most need in a certain moment: answers, abundance, soul connections or life changing situations. Synchronicity happens spontaneously and often unexpectedly. And here is where people have a challenge – letting go of timing.

I want you to think about one of your dreams. Imagine it's manifestation, see the perfect outcome for yourself. Bring in the feeling of accomplishment.

Now ask yourself, "Am I ok, even if my synchronicity happens 10 years from now?"

Your perfect relationship, your dream job, your new project... are you ok, if it happens in its own time? If you are, then you're in the best possible place of allowing.

• CHAPTER 3 •

Telepathy and Inter-species Communication

I WAS SO EXCITED. I had just bought a plane ticket to Azores, a group of islands in the middle of Atlantic, home to more than 30 species of whales and dolphins. It had been a year since my first dolphin swim in Hawai'i and I was ready to experience the bliss of seeing them underwater again. I was so excited!

But the dolphins had other plans. They somehow found a huge, multidimensional mirror and made sure to transmit the message of the masters to me, the message I talked about in the first chapter, "Look inside!"

I didn't get it. I couldn't see it coming. How could I? I was very naive. My logic was childlike, I thought it was a 3-step process, "I swim with dolphins. I experience bliss. I do it again." Nothing wrong with that, is there?

I should have known something was up when my dreams suddenly changed. It had been 6 years of the same recurring dream: seeing the dolphin fins and telling people about it. Now a new dream appeared, and it had a very, very different energy to it. Even though circumstances weren't the same every time, there was a common theme, a theme so strange, I didn't even know what to think of it: Dolphins and whales were starting to come to land!

They were climbing up cliffs, they were beaching themselves in front of me, intentionally and playfully, while I was walking on the sand. And whales were even using special strollers to move around my town, riding down the streets, pushing themselves along with their pectoral fins. What was going on??

One of the dreams was especially vivid, and it also carried another layer of information. I'm not sure if I can say, "I experienced enlightenment in my dreams," but it sure felt like it.

I am strolling along the edge of a tall cliff overlooking a wide bay. As I look across the water dolphins appear in the middle of the bay. I observe them and eagerly anticipate their next move. They start swimming towards me and I notice they are a different color, deep blue and yellow. As they near the cliff, some of them speed up and leap out of the water to land on rocky shelves. It becomes a game, where dolphins are trying to climb higher and higher towards me. One of them is especially determined and climbs half way up the cliff.

I continue with my walk and as the path nears a curve, I notice there's a short wall on the edge of the cliff. I stop and wonder if what I'm seeing is real – three dolphins are waiting for me on top of the wall. They must have climbed all the way up the cliff! The one that I was paying special attention to before is right in front, just lying there and looking at me. I approach him and without any thought, I place my hand on top of his beak. A bright explosion fills my third eye and I expand with the speed of light. I become the Universe. I am one with creation.

It seems obvious to me now, looking back, but at the time I had no idea what the dreams were trying to tell me. Luckily, I didn't have to wait long to find out. My next dolphin experience, contrary to my expectations, happened on land. In a kitchen to be specific.

Unexpected Transformation

"Hey, what about a hitch-hiking trip to the Croatian coast?" I was lying with a dear friend in a shade of a big, old cherry tree, enjoying summer laziness. We were daydreaming and brainstorming ideas about what to do in the next few weeks before I would fly to Azores.

"Dipping my toes in the Mediterranean Sea?" I thought. What a great idea! If you've never been to Croatia, it is Europe's second Greece: rugged, rocky coast with numerous small, romantic bays and inlets. Dozens of islands with crystal clear waters. Small fishing villages and long-forgotten city walls, built by Venetians at the peak of their empire.

"Sounds perfect. Do you want to go anywhere in particular?" I inquired.

"I have a friend in Rovinj you have to meet," my friend replied. "She is like a mermaid. Her husband is a fisherman and sometimes, while out on the ocean, dolphins come to their boat and play with a ball."

And so it was, that I came to meet Marinella, who was a catalyst for my dolphin transformation, as described in the introduction. I morphed, changed form, body part by body part. It is the most mystifying event of my life to this day. I came to town to see dolphins... and I met myself, as a dolphin!

That's when I remembered my dreams. I was speechless as the clarity of that metaphor was revealed to me. They are coming on land – through us!

What does that mean? How can I be both a human and a dolphin? Was this experience just for me or for other people as well?

I wish there were simple answers to these questions. I see my transformation as a multidimensional riddle – there are numerous ways to look at it and understand its meaning. But what if the only way to really get it is to actually experience it yourself? I am writing this book, not just to explain the gifts dolphins carry, but also to invite you to discover those gifts within. I will talk much more about this in later chapters, where I will also present a journey through 7 dolphin points on the human body, called Inner Dolphin Awakening.

I knew what happened was profound and I trusted more would be revealed with time. I was counting on dolphins to show me the next step. Now, I was really eager to see what would happen in Azores. Maybe the meaning of my transformation would be discovered there?

I had a dream right before I left. The dream was about communication.

I am standing on a small peninsula that stretches out in the ocean, creating bays on left and right of me. Dolphins are playing in one of the bays and noticing me, they change their direction and swim towards me. As they approach they dive and swim underneath me and only now I realize there's a channel, like a pipeline, that connects the two bays underneath the peninsula. The last dolphin in the pod stops, lifts half of its body out of the water to come really close to my face and starts chirping and clicking, like he's having a heated conversation with me. It goes on for a while, and even though I don't understand his language, I am totally immersed in the sounds.

Like many times before, this dream revealed what my next adventure would bring – and I again didn't understand until after it happened. I was the unwrapping the first layer of the gift of my dolphin transformation. That summer I was introduced to telepathy and inter-species communication.

Azores

I must admit, I was kind of disappointed landing in Azores. As we approached these volcanic islands in the middle of the ocean, my cells were still vibrating with the experience of Hawai'i, remembering that gentle, loving embrace of Lemurian energy. I was subconsciously expecting that same feeling of Aloha, but instead I was greeted by a green land that felt unfamiliar and distant. It took a week for me to let go of what I wanted Azores to be, and to open to what it actually is. Then all the synchronicities and gifts started to rush in. Who would have thought that a positive experience from the past could stop a benevolent flow in the present moment?

I landed on Sao Miguel, the main island and bought a ferry ticket that allowed for island hopping and ended up visiting five out of the nine islands in this beautiful chain. All the islands were incredible, they offered amazing views, hiking to lakes in craters of volcanos, snorkeling in lava tide pools and lots of fun meeting local people. Especially the island of Terceira etched into my memory as a place of soul connections.

When I came to the island of Pico though, I understood why dolphins and whales choose this place in the highest numbers. A perfectly shaped volcanic cone is rising from sea level all the way up to 7680 feet and appears from other islands like a huge pyramid. It carries a powerful energy and I spent my days on Terceira just looking at its majesty.

Risso's Love

"I want you all to keep your eyes open, ok?" spoke our skipper, as he gently guided our little boat past the volcanic cliffs and western slopes of Pico. "We have quite a few species of dolphins here. Most commonly we swim with bottlenose and spotted dolphins, but anything is possible."

I spotted a small town in the distance where the shore created a bay that, generations ago, became home to a little fishing village. As we were looking towards the village, something glistened in the water in front of us. Was that a fin? We held our breath. And there it was, a fin popped out again, followed by two more. Dolphins!

"They are Risso's dolphins." said our skipper, his face not revealing if that was a good thing or not. I had never heard of Risso's dolphins before, so I was eager to see what they looked like.

We neared them, slowly and gently. I loved how our skipper didn't want to force anything and allowed for 10-15 minutes of observing time. He wanted to make sure their behavior was welcoming, that they would keep on coming up for air close to the boat and not just swim off. The dolphins were keeping their course, not at all disturbed by us following along.

They had an aura of peace around them and their deliberate deep breaths were relaxing me. I counted nine different fins. I also noticed their different color, they were gray turning white in a way that almost looked like somebody had been scratching their gray color off to reveal white underneath. I later learned they turn whiter as they age. Unlike other dolphins, they have a short and round beak.

"Ok, we're going in," decided our skipper as he sped up a little and created a few hundred feet between us and the dolphins. "Two people at a time, no jumping or splashing, just gently slide in."

We were far from the shore and the water was too deep to see the bottom. Sun rays were piercing through infinite blue everywhere I looked. It was cold, and my body shivered as I took the first few strokes. I heard a loud exhale to my left and witnessed four Risso's dolphins, taking a breath and diving down to swim underneath me. It was so spellbinding to see white dolphins, like characters from a fairytale manifesting in front of my eyes.

Something shifted in me as I kept up with their pace. My body wanted to move like they do, mimicking the wave like motion of their tails. My hands stretched outwards and locked into a position of pectoral fins. Simultaneously I felt my heart open and love started to flow towards my sea cousins.

And that's when one of them turned on his back, revealing his underside, and kept swimming that way. This position was so intimate and trusting. We were mirroring each other, open heart to open heart. An invisible cord, like a soft laser light, formed between us. A beautiful presence enveloped me, embraced me, almost like I found myself inside his heart.

What intrigued me, was that I didn't only feel connected to one of them, but all four at the same time – as if they were one being. And that's when I suddenly understood the "pod mind." Dolphins are always both: individual and collective. Everyone in the pod knows everything that happens with the others, instantly. When I'm sharing a magical moment with one of them, the whole pod is aware of it. You could compare that to receiving a passionate kiss. Even though your lover only touches your lips, a wave of pleasure spreads throughout your body, arousing every cell.

I was excited with this new discovery. The dolphins had moved on, but the heart connection stayed. I started to wonder, if, by sensing the heart of one dolphin, I can tap into the collective heart of the pod, and thus witness the beauty of love they share between themselves?

As if wanting to answer this question, the rest of the pod approached me, and instead of diving down, they swam straight towards me. Five Rissos, four white adults and one gray baby, closed in on me until only a couple of feet away and then they gently veered off. As they did that, each one of them turned sideways, showing me their underside, opening their heart.

I was totally stunned, my arms open, my heart just receiving the immensity of their love. I could almost hear them say, "Welcome. Receive the gifts of our hearts," as this procession rolled on in front of my eyes.

The bliss I experienced in that moment was not of this world. I cried tears of gratitude. I was touched beyond words. Time and space ceased to exist. My heart stretched out into infinity, and it was filled with wonderful, sweet love. I was stoned, blissfully stoned, swimming in the sea of Risso's love.

Telepathy Happens Through the Heart

When I speak publicly about my journeys with cetaceans, I often say that I feel like they have many gifts in store for us, but we can only receive them when we're ready. It's almost like dolphins feel into us to judge when it's time to deliver the next insight, the next energetic download, a broader opening of the heart.

Immersing myself in the love and vastness of the Risso's heart was an experience that forever changed me. I felt like I was initiated into a pod, and as a new member I was gifted an insight into some of their secrets. I was eager to see what else would be revealed.

I booked another trip out, but this time our group was bigger and the whole excursion had a completely different energy. People on the boat were all young and had a party vibe to them, I was missing the peacefulness of the skipper from the last trip. Instead of Risso's, it was bottlenose dolphins this time and they seemed to reflect our energy – they were very active and swam past us quickly. I tried to connect with them but before I could really get in "the zone" they were gone, every time.

I was kind of annoyed as I watched them disappear in the distance and said in my mind, "Wait! Come back!" To my surprise one of the dolphins turned around and started to swim straight towards me. I was just resting on the surface, my arms open, ready for the meeting. My intuition was telling me the bottlenose would approach me, and we would start dancing and mimicking each other. I was ready! But when he was about 6 feet away I noticed, out of the corner of my eye, one of my co-snorkelers coming from the side. He swam straight into the bottlenose, almost like he wanted to collide with him. Dolphin veered off and turned around, meeting my eyes with a confused look, almost like trying to say, "Sorry mate, it's not working." And he was gone.

I was both upset with the person, and amazed by the fact that dolphin literally heard my thoughts and turned around... Let me point out that in every Azores encounter, before and after, dolphins always just swam one way, past us, underneath us, or around us... always keeping their course, except for this one dolphin. He did something completely out of the ordinary and it coincided with me asking him to do it. Was this a form of telepathy, inter-species communication?

I was quick to forgive my co-swimmer, since he hadn't really received proper training. How could he know that his actions and his energy were going to determine the quality of his dolphin encounter? He just wanted to get closer. Typically, it's all about getting the best photo, not understanding that dolphins will perceive this as aggressive behavior and vanish in a second. I hope one day, energy alignment, and respectful, loving approach are taught at the beginning of every dolphin tour (and the tour companies might realize they have more customers because of it too).

This experience also led me to gain a new understanding of group energy. Who are we as "human pod?" It doesn't necessarily matter if I'm aligned, if the group I'm a part of, is not. "Pod mind" doesn't just apply to dolphins, they experience humans as a pod as well. Which means they relate to our group energy as much as to an individual. It makes sense, doesn't it? And it stands as a reminder of what many wise teachers taught over the years: Be conscious of who you choose as your company.

Now, coming back to telepathy, here is my simple explanation of how it works: Yes, dolphins can read your thoughts, but your heart, your love, is the carrier. Which means telepathy is only possible when you're in love with someone (or something) first! Love builds a bridge between hearts and only then can thoughts travel over that bridge. That's why you always hear of people reading the minds of their loved ones and pets. It goes through the heart!

What is your alignment?

I just want to take a moment here to acknowledge our uniqueness, meaning each one of us will find our way into alignment in our own way. I want to stress the importance of dedication. Be willing to drop what's not important in your life and follow your intuition, your dreams, your excitement! It is only in the space of alignment that the universe responds in support, bringing about synchronicities and miracles.

Alignment played a large part in my last, unexpected encounter with dolphins in Azores. Like I mentioned in the first chapter, one way for me to align is to receive the wisdom and love from the other side. On the ferry ride back to the main island of Sao Miguel, I was sitting and listening to Kryon.

At one point, I felt myself expand outward, relaxing into the loving embrace of the Universe. I felt immense gratitude for everything that had happened in last weeks and sent my love to the waters surrounding us. A few minutes later I looked through the window and saw fins out on the water, swimming towards our ferry. I turned towards the rest of the sitting area, with a big smile, wanting to tell everyone dolphins were with us. But the passengers were lost in their own worlds: on their devices, sleeping; no one even met my eyes. I looked back out just in time to observe the dolphins diving down to swim underneath our ferry. In that moment, I understood: They'd come just for me, in response to my alignment. A special little gift, a farewell to their brother in a human form. I poured my love for them into words, "Thank you so much! I am forever blessed and forever changed by the gifts you brought to me! And thank you, Azores! (Even though you're not Hawai'i, you're not so bad after all.)"

Story of a Whale Who Heard Me

This story was floating around and searching for a place to land in this book. Even though it happened many years after my journey to Azores, I decided to include it here because of the telepathy connection. This story recounts an amazing inter-species communication that happened while I was on land!

There's a lovely, little bay on the Oregon coast, called Depoe Bay. It has a small town on top of the cliff and a little inlet, which makes for a very protected boat launch and fishing dock. Depoe Bay is famous for whale-watching. Little boats depart the dock and travel a couple of miles out to find Gray whales, who feed on amphipods, tiny shrimp-like animals who live in sediment on the ocean floor. You can stand on a cliff and look out across the horizon and sooner or later you'll spot a white splash, a powerful exhale from a whale's blowhole. While this is a fascinating sight in itself, you can get even luckier and see a whale enter Depoe Bay and come much closer to the shore.

And so it was, that one day I was standing on a cliff with my wife and we noticed a blow right in the middle of the bay. I felt a rush of excitement, as we watched the whale take a few deep breaths before diving back down. My consciousness traveled to meet with him, heart to heart. I then did something unexpected, I asked the whale to come closer. I drew an energy line on the surface, starting from where he was, coming across the bay right to the cliff where we were standing. I then totally released all expectations.

Shortly after, we watched in amazement as the whale slowly moved, periodically diving down to feed and re-surfacing every few minutes. To my complete astonishment, he was following the line I had drawn. Ten minutes later, he resurfaced right under our cliff, so close it seemed too shallow to allow for his immense size. He was maybe 20 feet away from the rocks, at the end point of my imaginary energy line! We were cheering and enjoying the beauty of this stunning moment, when an older couple joined us on the cliff and started to intently look across the ocean far away.

"There's a whale right here," I said with the biggest smile ever.

"Oh, we know, we've been watching them all day," said the guy, while he kept on looking across the horizon.

"No... there's a whale right here," I tried again, pointing to the shallow waters right under the cliff. In that moment, the whale came out for air again – and the couple started to scream,

"Oh my God, oh my God, oh my God, where's my camera?"

We were all laughing out loud.

The whale stayed in that one spot for five more minutes and then slowly started to move out towards the middle of the bay again. We were all gifted with the magical close encounter. I didn't tell anyone about my communication, I just silently sent my gratitude and love, and couldn't stop smiling all day.

When I share this story, people often ask me, "So you can call the whales? Let's go to the beach and you can get the whales to come to us." I have to disappoint them. None of what I did came from my mind at all. It was like a different part of me took over and my human self was a silent observer. Heart connection is the key, everything else happened in a world beyond. If I tried to do it again, it wouldn't come from a spontaneous, intuitive impulse; my mind would want to try to control and influence what happens. I believe this kind of synchronicity only happens when you completely and absolutely let go of any attachment and expectation, and connect heart to heart, guided by your higher self.

Exercise 3: Practicing Telepathy

This is one of my favorite exercises that I do as a part of my workshops. It requires two people, so go find a friend or a family member. Actually, I think your favorite pet, or a plant, may work just as well.

Sit across from each other and just take a couple of deep breaths to relax. Now, although you're doing this with another person, you will first send a thought to yourself. Close your eyes and say to yourself, "I allow myself to be everything I am." Observe how that makes you feel. Now open your eyes and send the same thought silently to the person (pet, plant) next to you. "I allow you to be everything you are." and then add, "I bless you!"

This is the beginning of building a bridge between the hearts. If you can go further and say, "I love you. Thank you for being here!" then go ahead. Every message you send has to be true for you in that moment. That's why at workshops I don't try to push people into loving somebody they've just met. But eventually, coming from a space of pure love will create a bridge between the hearts. And then telepathy will occur naturally. Have fun exploring!

• CHAPTER 4 •

Dolphin Assisted Therapy

A FEW YEARS AGO, I was blessed to have dinner with a well-known writer and she told me "the secret" to having your book be a bestseller.

"You must include 3 things," she said… "Romance, sex and death."

I was speechless. How in the world am I going to do that when my experiences with dolphins are all about bliss, joy and love? No one dies in this story. Dolphins do love to have sex, but that's not the point of this book. And romance, well, the invitation is to fall deeper in love with yourself. Does that count as romance? Then we come to a chapter like this one, where I will have to use a boring phrase like "final thesis." Did I lose you already, dear reader? Sleeping yet?

Joking aside, I trust that the words and energies presented here are going to find the right ear. And maybe one day we can change the paradigm. One day words written with a smile, talking about joy and love, can become a bestseller too!

After returning from Azores, I was determined to somehow connect my studies in social work with something exciting, and I found a mentor who approved my working title: "Dolphin Assisted Therapy and Social Work." To be honest, I had no idea what I was going to write about, because when you are in the academic world, you have to be, well, academic. Which means reviewing all the previous research, scientific articles, and studies. While reading about history of dolphin therapy was very educational, I didn't resonate with dolphins being kept in captivity and trained to act in a certain way for the purpose of therapy.

My interest, really, was in researching the effects of swimming with dolphins in the wild. No training, no instructions, no predetermination. What happens for people when they are out with a pod in the ocean? Can that be used in Animal Assisted Therapy, Psychology and Social Work?

Like Christopher Columbus I set sail to discover a new land, and at the same time, I knew that land already existed; I'd seen it with my own eyes. So, I must admit, although I tried not to be, I was biased from the beginning, already deeply in love with cetaceans. That's why I decided my thesis was not going to be scientific research that follows rigorous standards and routines (also called quantitative research), but more of an exploration into the personal, subjective experience of people who have met with dolphins in the wild for the first time (a.k.a. qualitative research). I chose stories over numbers, quality over quantity.

Myths, Stories and Legends

Getting to work, i.e. reading everything that was ever written about dolphins, I should have guessed there would be a few surprises in store for me. One of them had my jaw drop in a particularly big way. The ancients, aboriginal people of many lands, had stories that not only resembled, but literally described, my experiences!

First, I noticed, while studying the history of the human-dolphin connection, many ancient cultures had high reverence for the cetaceans. In many tribes, they were seen as omens of good luck; representing excitement and joy. In ancient Greece and Sumeria, dolphins were considered messengers from the Gods. We can read about many accounts of cetaceans helping sailors, the most well-known being the story of a Greek captain Arion, who was almost murdered by his crew, but managed to jump overboard in a moment of desperation and was saved by riding a dolphin to shore. To commemorate that event, he built a statue of dolphin rider.[1]

We can find a similar legend on the other side of the world, in New Zealand. "The Whale Rider" became world famous when it was nominated for an Academy Award in 2002. In the movie the story of Paikea is told, an ancestor to the tribe, who was traveling in his canoe across the ocean to settle Aotearoa (New Zealand). In a storm his canoe turned over and Paikea was sure to die, until the whales appeared and brought him to land. He became known as the whale rider.

"What an interesting metaphor," I thought to myself, "What does it mean?" Since I like my readers not to be bored to sleep, I hereby invite you, to breathe in the image of a dolphin/whale rider. Feel its underlying energy and see if you get any insights. Could it be it's a symbol representing unity and cooperation between two species? Or is there more? What if it also carries codes of remembrance, not of something outside of us, but a process within us? A human riding a dolphin. Take a deep breath and notice what your inner wisdom tells you (and we'll come back to this later, in chapter 6).

Then, exploring even further, I stumbled upon my main discovery: stories of morphing, shape-shifting and telepathy! Accounts from islands in Micronesia tell of dolphins changing into humans to watch islanders dance and sing. Similarly, I read stories from the Amazonian rainforest of pink dolphins believed to be able to change into human form and considered taboo, sacred and untouchable. But the biggest goosebumps were flowing up and down my spine as I read about Aboriginal tribes in Australia, some of them believing their lineage comes from the sea – they believe they were once dolphins who turned into humans!

Jasson Cressey, a Canadian author and lecturer, has published an amazing compilation of dolphin stories, myths and legends in his book, "Deep Voices: The Wisdom of Whales and Dolphin Tales."[2] Among the many stories, he speaks of the "Dolphin Tribe" of Mornington Island in Australia. As Jason explains, "The tribe has a shaman, who apparently has the ability to communicate telepathically with local dolphins, and the people believe that the shaman is a dolphin spirit that has chosen to reincarnate in a human body. Having the 'soul' of a dolphin, the shaman always understands the clicks and whistles of the dolphins and will always begin communicating with the dolphins using these sounds until, having built up the crescendo of dolphin chatter, both he and the dolphins suddenly fall silent. According to the shaman, it is at this point that the communication becomes telepathic."[3]

You can imagine the look on my face reading these words. After years of exploring by myself, I found someone else with a very similar story – and that someone was a shaman from the other side of the world!

And there was more. Jason continued to describe a special relationship that Aboriginal people have with cetaceans. There are many stories of fishing with the help of dolphins and sharing what was caught. A few tribes practice telepathic connection with dolphins and would even consult them about tribal matters. Such as the Wurunjeri tribe, who say the spirits of their deceased transform into dolphin bodies and guide them through life.

But perhaps the most interesting of these stories is the creation story of Groote Eylandt people of Northern Australia. The story is laced with metaphor and tells of the origin of their tribe. They say before people existed, there was a smaller kind of dolphin, led by Dinginjabana and his mate, Ganadja, who had a special relationship with shellfish. Diginjabana didn't approve of Ganadja's affection and attacked the leader of the shellfish. Ganadja knew that shellfish would call for aid and they did; the tiger sharks were summoned. The dolphins, being small, were no match for the tiger sharks and were all killed, except for Ganadja, who was saved by shellfish covering her body, hiding her out of sight. Here is where the story gets good. The souls of the killed dolphins rose from the ocean floor onto the land and became humans. Ganadja, who was the only one left in the ocean, gave birth to a different kind of a dolphin; bigger and stronger, as we know it today. Then she joined with Dinginjabana on land. They had many children who became the "Dolphin Tribe of the Groote Island". The tribe celebrates their special connection with their sea cousins to this day.

I believe this creation story carries many hidden meanings and metaphors, some clearer than the others. We witness a big shift, a change of the old ways, that gives birth to a humanity with a soul and a new kind of a dolphin. Has something happened in our past that altered both humans and the cetaceans and created a special connection between us? Humanity carries the soul of a dolphin. What does this mean? Is this a metaphorical or literal?

Chapter 6, titled "Explanations and Explorations," will attempt to answer some of these questions. Have I ever told you how hard it is to write a multidimensional book? Everything synchronizes and the stories, wisdom, explanations and even dolphins themselves, float around in my energy field together. The book already exists as an inter-connected whole, which can't be broken down. And yet my job is to organize it in a linear fashion, into chapters and pages, words, and sentences. So here I am, in Chapter 4, asking questions that can only be answered in Chapter 6. All I can do is smile, ask for patience, and invite you to become multidimensional as well.

Although I never doubted that what happened to me was real, similar stories from different tribes were the first outside confirmation. Which filled me with excitement and a feeling of belonging. All these accounts echoed within my being; a voice from the distant past, a whisper of the ancients saying, "You are not alone. We too knew about a special connection between humans and dolphins. What happened to you goes deeper than you think. Keep digging. There's more."

Synchronicity Aligns

After months of reading and reviewing the scientific articles, I was quite ready for another adventure. It was time to design my research. I must admit, all this academic stuff had me kind of lost in the world of the mind. I wrote to numerous places that do Dolphin Therapy and either got negative replies or a request for thousands of dollars that I didn't have. Then one day it dawned on me, I don't need to go to a center where dolphins are in captivity, I can explore what happens with dolphins in the wild! My heart started beating faster. Suddenly, I knew where I was going: Lemuria!

As this clarity emerged, doors opened, money showed up, resources aligned. I somehow even found a way for European Union Internships Fund to pay for my plane ticket to Hawai'i. Additionally, my mentor was completely supportive and fond of how I was designing my research. I felt like the wind was at my back and it truly seemed like the Universe was conspiring to help me achieve my dreams. It was magical.

Landing back in the land of Aloha felt as restorative and soul-nourishing as the first time. But now, I was on a different kind of mission. I first did a social work internship on the rainy side of the Big Island and then joined a week-long dolphin swim intensive with Joan Ocean in South Kona.

"She's kind of strange," were the words of my friend with a PhD, whom I had asked to help me formulate the questions for the qualitative research. She was sitting behind a computer, looking at Joan's webpage with a perplexed, almost worried look on her face, continuing, "I mean, she speaks about ETs and stuff."

I couldn't help but laugh out loud. I tend to forget how scared people get of the "woo-woo stuff." On the other hand, I've noticed a big shift in humanity in last ten years, where speaking about extraordinary things, including ETs (I prefer to call them star sisters and brothers), has become acceptable. There seems to be a general consensus, whomever I speak with agrees: there has to be intelligent life out there.

If you never heard of Joan Ocean, you may want to check her out.[5] She is a true pioneer in exploring the human-dolphin connection and I pay my deepest respects to her and everything she did throughout her life. Since the academic approach had me read all of the resources on cetaceans, I decided I should include books that really sparked my interest, which meant studying "oovy-groovy" Joan. After a few chapters I knew I needed to go see her and experience dolphins with her.

Joan began swimming with Hawaiian spinner dolphins in Kealakekua Bay in the 1980s. Back then, she was the only one out in the water with them. Living in a house next to the ocean, she would check the bay every morning and if dolphins were there, she would swim out and spend time with them. Over the years she logged thousands of hours in what she calls "participatory research." She wrote in a diary every day and published her experiences in two books, Dolphin Connection (1989) and Dolphins into The Future (1997). The concepts and teachings she presents are mind-blowing and heart-opening.

I decided it was time to dive into the sacred waters of Kealakekua Bay and see what life would bring me next.

Special Greeting

On the first day of the seminar, early in the morning before our gathering started, I was down in the bay, surrounded by a pod of spinner dolphins who blessed me with their presence. I'd brought a young couple I'd met at a hostel, but soon lost sight of them. It was one of those magical swims where it seems like you have a whole pod to yourself. A few dolphins swam underneath me, and I was immersing myself in the feeling of pod alignment. I swam at the same speed, above them, allowing my energy to merge with theirs. And that's when it happened, as I enjoyed looking at a pod underneath me, one of them left the group, swam up towards the surface, accelerated and propelled himself out of the water, spinning in the air. He did it four times, each jump landing closer to me. When on the last jump, he ended up just a few feet away and did something unusual: he positioned his body vertically, looking me in the eyes, almost like he wanted to greet me 'standing up.' I was taken aback, time seemed to stop, while he stayed in that posture for a good five seconds before swimming off.

When I mentioned this in our opening circle Joan playfully giggled and added, "Their jumps are their way of saying 'hello' and 'goodbye' and you've experienced a very special greeting."

Silently thanking the dolphins, I thought to myself, "I wonder how great this seminar is going to be, if their welcome was so cool?" I looked around the room and noticed how our entire group of participants had a warm and welcoming glow. "Before I forget," I heard myself blurt out, "I am doing a research and would appreciate if I could interview you all about your experiences." The support was there. Everyone was excited about my thesis, and more than happy to help me.

Be Joyful

The following week was filled with dolphin swims in the mornings and meditations/sharing circles in the afternoons. There were two experiences that really stood out for me. The first was a very clear telepathic communication, that could very simply carry the cetaceans' most important message to humanity. It happened on the second day of the seminar, one that was abundant with cetacean encounters. The dolphins' energy was both peaceful and exuberant and they loved interacting with everybody, spreading us out in the water and having lots of fun with us. Even though I immensely enjoyed the whole interaction I couldn't help but notice spinners were coming very close to almost everyone else but me, for some reason they kept me at a distance. The longer we were in the water with them, the more this nagged at me. You know that silly thought, that enters your brain and doesn't want to leave you alone? Why wouldn't they want to come and see me up close?

I was diving down, swimming fast, swimming slow, lying on the water, allowing, joining with others, swimming alone... whatever I did, the dolphins stayed away from me. As I was watched everyone else have amazing encounters, my frustration grew. In one moment, I said in my mind, "Dolphins, why are you staying away? What do I have to do?" And that's when I heard it, loud and clear inside me, "Be joyful!"

Our minds are tricky, they make us base the value of our experience on what we perceive physically, when in fact, other levels of perception are more important. I always tell people that you may have the most powerful experience with dolphins swimming deep underneath, where you can hardly see them, a transfer of energy and communication could happen with a force that will knock your socks off (or your fins in this case). Time and space don't matter, state of mind, state of heart is the only thing that matters, so be joyful!

We climbed back on our boat soon after and I just did it, I became joyful... with other people! I surprised myself, my main intention until that moment was to be with dolphins and I didn't really take time to have fun with people. After hearing the spinners' message, I opened up and out started to flow laughter, silliness and jokes. My feeling of connection went from fifty percent to a hundred and ten percent, and suddenly, I felt like I was a part of a family; like I'd known everyone for years. Most importantly, that's when I stopped being attached to how my next swim with dolphins would go – because I was already joyful.

As you know, when you release expectations, everything comes to you. My next time in the water, our sea cousins were all around me. My joy was recognized and felt. And not just that, something magical happened when our swim was complete. Everyone had already climbed onto the boat and I was the last one left in the water, as I tried to swim around the boat to the stairs to emerge, the captain said with a smile, "Look in the water... and don't take too long."

You know how people crave that special moment, when a dolphin locks eyes with you, swimming by your side, creating a feeling of union and oneness? Well, when I looked in the water, a single dolphin was there, just waiting for me. I looked into his eyes and he started circling around me, with his loving, wise gaze never leaving mine. I followed him, and we spun, ever so gently, allowing for everything else to dissolve. With that graceful dance, time and space disappeared into a long-forgotten universe and everything but us ceased to exist. Beauty and presence. Wonder and gratitude. A special gift for a human that embodied the simplest yet most profound cetacean message, "Be joyful!"

Human Dolphins

The second gift of that week was discovering I was not alone. Realizing that shamans on the other side of the planet believed they were dolphins in a human body was one thing but meeting human-dolphins in person took my journey to a whole new level. Until that moment, I never even considered others having similar experiences. But think about it, if dolphins come in pods then human-dolphins come in...?

Hanging out with Joan I couldn't help but attentively observe her smile, her eyes, her face, her gestures. There was a warm familiarity that I couldn't quite put my finger on. Especially her giggles, they resonated somewhere deep inside me, like I was remembering a dream, but I couldn't recall all the details. And then, a couple of days into the seminar, it hit me: she's a dolphin! It couldn't have been any clearer. She completely embodied their playfulness, joy, and curiosity. What a beautiful thing to witness. And how amazing to meet another dolphin in human form!

The third day of the seminar was a day off, and Nicki, my "dive buddy," and I, spent it driving to different bays, snorkeling and having fun.

At one point, I turned to her and said, "You know, I actually am a dolphin."

"You too?" was her reply, laughing. "Tell me about it!"

I shared my experience with Marinella and then she described a very similar story, followed by her frustration when morphing happened in the least appropriate places. "For example, coming here, I was standing in line at the airport, when my dolphin came out and became extremely interested in baggage screening and what all those electronics and monitors were about... It was so hard to stay in line!"

Now, years later, after traveling the world, I've met quite a few people who know of their dolphin connection and many more who have it in them and are not consciously aware of it – they just follow what feels good, gifting everyone they meet with their giggles and excitement. The question that these encounters bring out for me is: What if we all have a dolphin inside us, a place of joy, curiousity, and playfulness, and all we need to do is open to it?

The Interviews

On the last day of the seminar I started with interviews. I wanted to be very general with my questions, allowing for personal experiences to be shared. I was interested in what the difference was (if any) between swimming in the ocean alone or snorkeling in the ocean with dolphins. Was their experience physical, emotional, mental, or spiritual? What else happened that was of importance to them?

As tends to happen with science, I had a nice bell curve of normal distribution, experiences ranging from "amazing" and "mind-blowing" to "kind of disappointing." But one thing really stood out: the biggest impact, for almost everyone, happened on an emotional level. Dolphins brought a sense of joy, peace, excitement and celebration. Not only that, they acted as motivation as well, two of the participants conquered their fear of water. One of them was afraid of water her whole life, so scared she had a hard time washing her hair while showering. Dolphin love brought her from Canada to Hawai'i and in one week, she overcame her fear to such a degree, she was able to snorkel with us, swim in the ocean without seeing the bottom and absolutely enjoy her time with the spinners. She said the love she felt for dolphins was stronger than the fear – and that was her path to freedom.

The one person, who was "kind of disappointed," flew all the way from Australia to experience what she imagined would be the most special moment of her life – a dolphin would swim by her side, looking into her eyes... and it never happened. The dolphins stayed at a distance and no matter what she did she could never get them to come close. Sounds familiar? When listening to her, I couldn't help but to notice how our expectations limit our experience. Because something doesn't happen we feel unfulfilled and disappointed. Letting go of expectations is the key. Understand that dolphins are multidimensional beings, who can interact with you across great distances. When you're ready to receive, the gift will come to you, even if you're thousands of miles away.

All the participants seemed to agree that swimming with dolphins had a much greater impact on them than just swimming in the ocean. While experiencing a feeling of relaxation when snorkeling with fish and coral, dolphins bring in a special presence. One that touches many levels of the human being, and brings about a strong emotional response, and for some people, even a feeling of bliss.

Another interesting thing that many people shared, was how they experienced Joan. They said that their encounters with Joan were as inspiring as their dolphin swims. They felt her dolphin-like attitude, the way of being that she embodied, was something they could take back home and implement into their daily lives. They felt inspired to become dolphin-like too, to become a joyful human!

I did a follow up 3 months later, as I was wondering how much of people's experiences in the seminar could be integrated into their daily lives? Was the emotional change still there? What else had happened that they felt was significant?

Most people, including me, went through a period of emptiness after getting home. You could say being in Hawai'i with dolphins was so colorful that the routine of everyday life seemed gray, not interesting. This feeling brought about a space of being neither here or there, a struggle between an old and a new self. How to birth dolphin joy into everyday reality? Some people experienced this empty space as depressing, it hit them harder than they expected. It seemed the key to finding their way out of it was to discover new ways of expressing and creating: some started to write a diary and paint; others put dolphin photos on their walls, to serve as a reminder. Most of the interviewees felt they were partially or fully successful in integrating what happened. Even the lady who was originally disappointed was taking Joan's example of joyful living and implementing it in her women circles.

Hearing the experiences of others helped me accept my own. Coming back to Slovenia from Hawai'i was made harder by the change of seasons. Winter began, and I struggled with trying to find any excitement in the gray weather. I was reminiscing about the openness and joy I had felt just a few months before. Although I did many things that would usually make me happy, I felt an underlying emptiness, a feeling of detachment. I felt like I left a big piece of myself in Hawai'i and was trying to figure out how to bring it back, to the present moment. My answer came as Native American wisdom. I went to see a public talk by shaman Tim Sikyea, a native of the Lakota tribe who now lives in Germany and travels to Slovenia to hold sweat lodge ceremonies. He said one thing that really hit me, "In my tradition we share stories all the time. I was surprised seeing you Europeans hardly do it at all... You must take time to share a story. That's the only way for magic to happen, where one soul can touch another. And that's the only thing that really matters in life."

In that moment, clarity descended up on me, "I have to share my story! I have to speak my truth. I have to create a space where a part of me, that's still in Hawai'i, can come here and start speaking about what happened on my journeys, expressing the truth – my truth!" At the same time, I knew (and this was kind of scary), that nothing could be held back. If I'm sharing what happened, I need to share everything, including the "strange stuff," like stories of morphing and telepathy. I sat down behind my computer and wrote, "Dolphin Evening: Jan's stories, photos and videos – experiences with dolphins from Hawai'i, Azores, Croatia and Australia."

Dolphin Evening

What is your biggest fear? Would you feel comfortable standing on stage sharing your light, your most intimate self? That's what Dolphin Evening was for me: stepping, yet again, through one of my biggest fears:

fear of enlightenment. Why would someone be afraid of enlightenment? Because, quite a few times when we've done it in the past, something bad happened. We were killed, tortured and persecuted for our gifts. We were seen as a threat to churches and governments. At the very least, we were "the strange ones," living by ourselves in a little cottage at the edge of the village; people would only come to see us when they needed our help. When a bad scenario plays itself out so many times, it starts to imprint itself onto your Akash in a very deep way. It's like a big part of you is constantly repeating, "Don't wake up to your light again." Your past incarnations are trying to protect you, like a mother wants to protect her child, thinking she knows what's best.

I didn't feel this fear at all until I started to wake up (see chapter 1). And then it seemed like every cell of my being started to shout at me, "What are you doing?! Hide! Stay normal! Don't show your light!!" The way this fear would descend on me was overwhelming – and completely irrational. There were times when I couldn't leave the house because, "they were waiting to get me," and other occasions when, attending a public event, I was sure the crowd was suddenly going to turn towards me and "hang me." These are all past life experiences that my cells could remember and needed to clear before I could really move on.

The problem was, whatever I tried (healers, techniques, workshops), didn't really release the fear. I had to invent my own approach, which is: Take a small step into the light, pause, and reassure yourself everything is ok... Repeat. It involves a lot of patience, talking to my cells and the courage to keep on doing it – despite the fear. There is a wonderful book written by Susan Jeffers (that I've never read because the title was enough), called, "Feel the fear and do it anyway." That was my journey over the years, slowly sharing more of myself, my truth, my light.

One of the biggest steps was when I began to give workshops, presenting tools for self-empowerment. First one person showed up ... *I didn't die.* Then three ... *still alive.* Then five... *starting to enjoy it, it would be a shame if they killed me now.* It was two steps forward and one step backwards for years. Sometimes I had periods of running away, trying to be "normal." But the light, my light, kept on calling me. My intuition was telling me, "You are safe. This lifetime is going to be different. You are safe." I used these words to talk to my cells whenever I emerged from my bubble. When everything went smoothly I would say to my body, "See, you were wrong. Nothing happened. They actually loved me. I am safe."

Slowly, bit by bit, the fear loosened its grip. I could see the changes in me, the way I shared myself, the way

I communicated. I was finding my voice, I was emerging into the light. Then came the Dolphin Evening. I was excited, organizing and preparing for a few weeks, and was honored when 20 people showed up. It felt so good to be standing on a stage, ready to tell the story of my journey. The moment before I opened my mouth was both exciting and scary. There was a familiar, and by now tiny, voice inside trying to talk me out of it. I acknowledged it, smiled, and started, "It all begins with a dream..."

What I shared was accepted with warmth, love, and appreciation. People came to me afterwards and wanted to share their stories, their love, their inspirations. And once more I could reaffirm to my cells, "I am safe!"

Another thing emerged as a part of that first event. A few days before it started I felt like I wanted to not only tell my story but for people to have their own experience as well. This inspired the playful creation of a few practical exercises with the intention of generating a feeling of dolphin connection – even for people who had never seen a dolphin before. In a way it was an experiment, I had no idea how it would work, and it turned out great. You could feel the energy in the room change with each exercise and many people shared afterwards how it was their favorite part. Now, looking back, I celebrate it as the beginning of Inner Dolphin Awakening. It started with one simple question, "What if everything you knew to be true about dolphins, was inside you?"

Back to Dolphin Therapy

Maybe some of you have read the chapter until this point and are saying, "Wait, I thought you were going to speak more about Dolphin Therapy. I want to hear how dolphins heal with their sonar."

Yes, a big part of my thesis was studying Dolphin Assisted Therapy: what happens, how it works, how it doesn't work, what was scientifically proven, etc. Please find links to some of the research on my website if this is of interest to you.

But here, I want to simply present my reflections on the subject as a whole.

Dolphin Assisted Therapy has had many wonderful results over the years. It also raised many questions and doubts, since dolphins were used mostly as positive reinforcement, meaning a treat for a job well done, a carrot on a stick.

It wasn't easy for me to dive deep into the subject, because until that moment all I had was my own personal experience with dolphins in the wild. My meetings were not scheduled, constructed, or organized in any specific way. So, you can imagine me reading about therapists working with dolphins in captivity, training them to act a certain way while trying to get a response from a child or disabled person... it seemed so contrived, downgrading the magnificence of what is possible into predictability and form. It was like taking a free-flowing formless dance master and teaching them steps for waltz (no offense to people that like to waltz). I know and understand, there can be gifts in that, but it certainly didn't feel like a path I wanted to tread, or simply put: It just didn't feel right!

And I wasn't the only one. Over the years, many centers have changed the way they keep dolphins in captivity. They have started to allow them to form pods and swim openly in a part of the ocean that's separated with nets. Probably the most well-known is Dolphin Reef Eilat in Israel, where they went a step further and have dolphins interact with swimmers on their own terms, meaning dolphins are not trained to pull you around or take happy photos with you. They are still in captivity, but with much greater freedom than most of the dolphinariums in Mexico, the Bahamas or Florida. Here's a short description of Dolphin Reef's therapy program, "The Dolphin Reef is a unique site in terms of the conditions in which the dolphins live and the Human-Dolphin relationships that are formed as the result of our way of interacting with them. The dolphins are able to maintain their social structure, living as a permanent group, and they are free to choose whether or not to approach any person who enters their world.

"The program "Supportive experience with the aid of dolphins" has existed since 1991 and was initiated by Sophie Donio, M.A. The program is suitable for children from 6 to 16 years old who face various challenges and mental difficulties with problems such as: Post-Traumatic Stress Disorder, Autism, Dyslexia, behavioral problems, Down-Syndrome, depression, cancer patients, and victims of sexual-abuse, among others.

"The concept and core of this program are to give the children an opportunity to experience positive moments and be themselves. The children feel, and respond to, the freedom given to them, so they more easily accept our working framework; they receive love so they become more open; they feel their success and they receive personal attention which makes them more confident; they receive strong emotional stimuli, which strengthens them; and they walk on the moving pier, which improves their movement and balance.

"Motivation is the word to describe what the Dolphin Reef is creating for the children in this program. When the children feel better about themselves, they become motivated to accomplish greater things."[6]

I've heard amazing stories about Eilat dolphins interacting with disabled kids in a unique way, like they knew and understood they could make a big impact on these children's lives. I congratulate Dolphin Reef on implementing a much more natural, dolphin-friendly way of keeping these creatures in captivity. If it has to be done at all, this should be the standard.

Exploring further I was truly happy and excited when I discovered Water Planet in Florida; to my knowledge the only place in the world, that offers Dolphin Assisted Therapy in the wild. Here's what they say about their program, "Water Planet's dolphin therapy programs use the emotional impact of a dolphin encounter in his own environment combined with expressive art, massage, cranio-sacral therapy and music as a beneficial experience for children with disabilities, emotionally challenged and fragile children."[7]

"Finally, somebody gets it," was all I could say. My soul was singing as I read the following passage from their webpage,

"A dolphin encounter in the wild is an extraordinary experience. The adventure of being face to face in the ocean with a large and wild air-breathing mammal is a powerful one that will not easily be forgotten and that is only given to a minority, especially in our society, where we are mostly living in a controlled environment without direct contact with the wilderness. A wild dolphin is a symbol of freedom. He triggers in us these feelings of joy, excitement, wonder, sometimes awe, even rapture for some. Therapy with dolphins deals with using the strong emotional release of this experience to disrupt social barriers and inhibitions."[8]

My question is: if people feel blissful with dolphins, is it possible to use that bliss to inspire a positive change in a person?

(Inner) Dolphin Assisted ~~Therapy~~ Empowerment

What really happens when people heal? Is it dolphins that heal humans? Or is it us allowing the fullness of our being again? I believe it is us. I believe dolphins help us to remember what we can do. I came to a point in my work, where I had to replace the word "Therapy" with the word "Empowerment," meaning a person waking up to powers that are already inside. Dolphins are an inspiration on that journey. That way, it stopped being a process of "Here's what the goal is and here's how we're going to get there," (therapy) and it became "An inner and outer journey of discovery of what is already a part of us." (empowerment)

I also added "Inner" in front of "Dolphin Assisted Empowerment". I believe we carry cetaceans inside. I'm teaching people how to tap into that part of themselves and integrate it just like they would integrate the blissful state of a dolphin swim. Of course, if the opportunity arises, seeing dolphins in their natural environment is still a valuable experience, but you can tap into the energy with your consciousness from wherever you are. You always have it right here, in every cell of your being.

Here is my take on dolphin healing: Dolphins embody joy, peace and bliss. They carry multidimensional understanding, not just of who they are, but who we are. They carry the Akash of the planet, so when they look us in the eyes, they not only see us as humans, they see our soul. They see the magnificence of a multidimensional being, filled with light, color and sound. They see our past and future incarnations and they understand the service we're doing for the planet and the Universe as we take on the veil of forgetfulness.

They don't react to this, but simply stay present with what they see. They feel an immense love and gratitude for our being and they understand that ultimately, everything is always ok. They know we can always return to our natural flow, we can always remember our magnificence. And sometimes they are overwhelmed with the beauty of it all. They want to say, "This is so amazing. You're so beautiful. Your journey is so inspiring." They simply cannot contain the pure joy of seeing us. That's when they swim erratically, jump and spin. “Let’s celebrate, dance and play together, dear human.” they say.

Your cells respond. Your whole being starts to remember. Your Akash opens and out pours the beauty of your soul. Your heart expands. You start to realize, you too, are the embodiment of joy, love, and bliss. This is the natural state of your soul. And in this state, anything can be healed. In this state, no limitations exist. In this state, you heal yourself!

• CHAPTER 5 •

The Journey of the Tones

WHILE EVERY JOURNEY BRINGS unique gifts, it is only certain journeys that are etched into your soul in a way that surpasses time and space. A journey like this creates a resonance that can be felt through many lifetimes and keeps on calling you into further expansion. The Journey of the Tones is the journey of my soul from the stars to planet Earth, it is an experience of Lemuria and the sacredness of a new beginning, it is a voyage across the great ocean to create a new home, and a celebration of many incarnations under the stars of the Pacific.

The Journey of the Tones called me again in this lifetime. The call came quietly at first, like a gentle whisper in the wind, "You are Lemurian, you are Lemurian." I heard those words every time Kryon channeled. For a couple of years, I was certain he called everybody Lemurian until I realized he only did it when channeling in Mount Shasta. That's where he also pulled Dr. Todd, part of the Kryon team, out of the audience in 2003 and revealed his Lemurian name was Yawee.[1] His Akash was profound. He was the greatest scientist of Lemuria who designed Temples of Rejuvenation, where Lemurians came to re-adjust their cellular age, which allowed them to live in a youthful body for hundreds of years.

I started to pay special attention to Dr. Todd Ovoykaitys' work after the 2003 Mt. Shasta channeling, and was especially attracted to Pineal Toning, an ancient way of using sound for balancing, healing and expanding awareness.[2] I had no idea toning would become a big part of my dolphin journey. Dr. Todd was at one point a conventional medical doctor who invented a "Qi laser," the first interdimensional device on the planet, according to Kryon. The laser has an amazing rejuvenating ability and carries quantum information, that reminds the cells of a natural state of perfect health.

Amidst years of scientific research with the Qi laser, Dr. Todd started to tone and produce funny sounds nobody could repeat. These sounds had the effect of opening people up to profound states of consciousness.

Dr. Todd calls the tones Pineal Toning, based on an ancient knowledge of the Pineal gland being the seat of the soul. Modern research shows toning increases the Pineal gland's beneficial hormonal activity.

In 2007, after I returned from Iceland, I spent the last of my money attending an event on EMF Balancing Technique in Germany. While enjoying what was presented someone casually mentioned, "And isn't it wonderful, Dr. Todd is coming here in two weeks to teach Pineal Toning?" What?! I had to go... But how? I was penniless! In a moment like this it's good to remember Bashar's definition of abundance, "Ability to do what you need to do when you need to do it." In other words, if you're meant to be somewhere, it will happen. I walked up to a stand selling books and asked a helper, "You don't have to pay to attend the event, do you?" She shook her head. "I want to volunteer when Dr. Todd is here!"

Michael, the organizer, listened to my story, smiled and said, "Sure, see you in 14 days." How easy was that? I was so grateful! I later learned that Michael had already had enough volunteers and made up a position just for me. I would be 'the water man" (wink from the Universe), responsible for filling up water cups during the break.

Learning the Pineal Tones was more profound than I had expected. Singing them in a group of 200 people was extremely powerful. I could feel the sound travel deep into inner dimensions I didn't even know existed. The tones felt ancient and yet strangely familiar, like they were a part of me. On the last day, Dr. Todd shared a tone he couldn't teach, he said. It was impossible to write it down and specify the phonetics. He learned it while he stayed in Maui and was free-diving. The sound was so beautiful he would dive to the bottom and hold onto a rock to stay underwater longer. It was the song that was, according to Aboriginal people, part of the creation of our world. It was the song of the whales!

We were invited to close our eyes and relax, and Yawee started to sing. I loved how the sound moved through my body and activated different parts of my skull. Sometimes deep and gurgly, other times high pitched and pulsating, whale song was simply out of this world and if it was the only thing I heard in those two days, it would have been enough to carry the whole weekend.

Whale song was the first connection between my love for cetaceans and my newly born passion for toning. Over the years this connection has strengthened and led me to discover how singing the tones to dolphins and whales creates pure magic. My two passions began to merge and become one multi-faceted journey, The Journey of the Tones.

A Message to The Stars

"The old souls who remember this ritual will be there. Collect them from all over the planet. It will be a celebration like no other."[3] These words from Kryon concluded his invitation to the Lemurian Choir in Maui, a unique gathering where Pineal Tones would be sung in pairs for the first time in 26.000 years. I was sitting at the back of a conference room in Lisbon, Portugal, when Kryon's invitation came on the screen. While reading I felt a huge, spinning ball of energy fly across the room and hit me in the chest. It was so powerful it almost knocked me over. As I was trying to breathe and allow the immensity of the energy to sink in, I turned to my neighbor and said, "I am already there." She just nodded, smiling. I knew with utmost certainty, that I was already in Maui, even though the event was almost two years away. So Kryon's words weren't really an invitation. They were a reminder of a contract that I had signed in joy, long before I even set foot on this beautiful blue planet.

Kryon said the Lemurian Choir was here to send a message to the Universe on December 21, 2012 stating,

"We made it. Humanity is not destroying itself. We are waking up and starting to remember the sacredness inside." He said the message is multidimensional and would be heard by anyone who had an ability to receive it – any civilization that is in full remembrance of their divine nature. The choir would do that by pairing the tones into specific harmonies, using what is in musical terms called "open fifth." By the time the choir started there would be 24 levels of Pineal Tones that would create 12 pairs. This ceremony wasn't new; we had gathered every winter solstice in Lemuria to send a message back to the Pleiades. Yawee brought the tones forth in that lifetime and was remembering them again this time around as Dr. Todd. The choir hadn't gathered since Lemuria sank, 26,000 years ago. December 21, 2012, was a demarcation of the shift, representing awakening of humanity. It was time for Lemurian choir to sing again.[3]

Reviewing all the synchronicities that brought me to that moment, I was astonished. I understood I was slowly being prepared for the choir without even knowing it was coming. I learned first eight toning levels in Germany in 2007, practicing them daily to slowly open up. I knew they were special and I loved immersing myself in the timeless space they created.

My journey to Hawai'i in 2009, was another piece of the puzzle. I got to be with the islands prior to the choir and had plenty of time to slowly assimilate everything I was feeling there. I began to call Hawai'i home during this time and every moment spent there allowed for more integration of my Lemurian self. By the time the choir started, I was able to stand there in full remembrance and sing my heart out in celebration.

And what are the odds I would have dreams about visiting Portugal for many years and when I finally chose to do a student exchange, in the spring of 2011, Kryon visited for the first time, presenting the invitation for the Lemurian Choir? I was in the right place at the right time.

Lemurian Reunion

"Ah-ee-oh, ah-ee-oh" reverberated through the air. The simple tune of toning level 24 was filling every cell with the sweetness of remembering. We were standing on a lawn, with the sounds of ocean surf in the distance. Trade winds danced around us as the first stars began to twinkle in the night sky. This was a reunion of not just the 900 of us who felt called to attend the Lemurian choir, it was a reunion with the ancient energy in the land that was waiting for us. There was a feeling of joy and celebration in the air. We thought we were going to send a message of, "We made it!" out into the Universe, but everywhere I turned I could hear that same message whispered back to me, 'You made it! Thank you. We celebrate you!" The land knew it. The ocean knew it. The trees knew it.

Singing the tones under the stars that night was supposedly a preview, "a dress rehearsal." The real event was to happen the next day, Winter Solstice of 2012, the last day of the Mayan calendar. But the feeling that night was nothing short of spectacular. The pieces of the puzzle were being put into place. It felt like slowly waking up from a dream. I observed a veil in my cells, like a dark overlay, slowly being lifted. Every tone vibrated that veil, to where it was becoming less stable and strong. And in flowed a remembrance of what was behind it, like a light shining through a crack in the door. That light was an understanding of my quantum nature. It was an understanding of how everything is both inside and outside of me. A knowing that the land, the ancestors and the tones also live within. Was I sending the message out to the Universe or was I awakening the layers of DNA that remember the Universe inside me? Kryon's answer to that is, "Yes!" The joy of remembering is so sweet and precious. It filled the cells with an inner smile as "Ah-ee-oh, ah-ee-oh" reverberated through the air. I was home.

The journey to get there hadn't been totally smooth. A few months before the choir I finished my studies, which was the last thing that bound me to the country where I was born. I felt that all my passions and aspirations for life in Slovenia were complete. I was ready to leave on a one-way ticket. The Pacific was calling me. The choir was just the beginning. I would spend three months in Hawai'i and then fly to New Zealand, where I was approved for a one-year work and holiday visa. And from there, who knew. While all this was exciting, there was one problem. I had a girlfriend I loved dearly, and even though we had often journeyed together in the past, she didn't want to travel anymore.

"It's not the first time you're doing this" said James,[4] a gifted healer from Colorado, when I told him about the journey ahead. "I see at least two past lives where you put your backpack on your shoulders and left. You just started walking. In one of those you traveled to the edges of the Roman empire while in another, you explored the green countryside of the British Isles and met a beautiful woman who you fell in love with, and you stayed with her. That love was so strong, you're still searching for her, lifetimes later. I suggest releasing her, so you can be fully present in your current relationship." I agreed. "Mysterious woman from a past life, wherever you are, I let you go."

While it brought peace to my heart, to know I was choosing my girlfriend fully, it didn't help her with accepting the fact that I needed to go. How do you explain that The Journey of the Tones is calling you? All I had was a feeling in my cells, deep ancient intuition, not just Lemuria, not just the tones, but pieces and parts of my past were reaching out to me... I didn't understand it at the time, but I had lived many lifetimes on different islands in Pacific and I was supposed to meet and merge with these energies from my past. Sometimes you have to put your feet on the land you used to call home to truly integrate that part of you. It's almost like you leave your essence in the rocks (and the ocean), to be picked up again, when the time is right.

Celebrating the Shift

"There's more." I heard those words from my spirit guides every time I expanded beyond what I'd thought was possible. They would say it in moments of gratitude, when I felt my heart was so full it could burst. They would say it in moments of fulfillment, when I thought my mission was done and there couldn't possibly be anything new for me to experience in this lifetime. And they said it that evening in Maui, when the "dress rehearsal" for Lemurian choir was over and I couldn't imagine how the event the next day could top it.

Trusting my guides, I showed up with excitement on December 21, 2012, to once again sing the tones so dear to my heart. Is it even possible to describe the feeling of sacredness and honor, when you're a part of a ceremony like that?

900 of us responded to the call. It had been 26.000 years since the tones had been performed in a choir. You can imagine the simple joy of souls reconnecting and hugging, after many lifetimes. Now add to that the energy of celebration within the group consciousness of humanity, that has chosen to wake up instead of going through Armageddon. Gaia, with dolphins and whales, is very aware of this shift. But the highest levels of excitement came from realities unseen: ancestors, guides, star people, and ancients. They can observe the beauty of the multidimensional picture and can feel the resonance our awakening creates. They were present with incredible love and honor, adding to our tones a song of celestial joy. Is it possible to describe the feeling in the room on that day? I don't know. All I can do is invite you to feel it for yourself. Breathe it in and know that we have entered a new time, one that has the potential for the highest consciousness humanity has ever seen (according to Mayan calendars that go past 2012). The

energy of that room was the beginning of something special that includes every one of us. So, thank you for reading these words and doing your work – embracing your soul and awakening to your quantum nature. It is important, and I celebrate you!

For me, performing the tones in the choir was the highest honor I could have received. I have no idea how large of a quantum ripple our toning created, but I felt the appreciation coming from so many sources, sacredness permeated the very building after we finished. It was a joyful job, a calling that was agreed upon by my soul eons ago. Standing there with hundreds of people, watching the heart coherence form over the days and feeling the immensity of energy behind the choir, was the greatest gift that life had bestowed on me.

Kryon channeled between different sets and said the irony was, we had no idea what we were really doing. He described it as "turning the key in the lock."[5] The lock was a quantum energy that was put there by Pleiadeans, waiting for that moment. The key were the tones and also the consciousness of humanity – nothing would have happened if we hadn't woken up. Turning the key is a symbol for opening the door to allow new energy to start flowing on the planet – which will assist in raising consciousness and bring forth new concepts, ideas, and inventions. Until that moment, the planet was isolated in a way that allowed for humanity's complete free choice between light and dark. From 2012 on, the planet is slowly starting to lean towards the light. It's almost like light, for the first time, makes more sense to people – especially to the young ones, who are born in this new energy. This new consciousness will eventually bring us to gentle solutions for some of our most difficult problems and for the most impactful shift – creating peace on Earth.

And then Kryon said something that had me lean forward and listen intently. He invited Dr. Todd not to stop now, to put the choir together in different places with specific intentions, one of them being: to sing to the cetaceans!

I decided to try that right away.

Singing to Cetaceans

Over the years, it has become my favorite thing to camp in one of the dolphin bays on the Big Island. I adore the feeling of excitement when I wake up at 6am and start unzipping my tent, to peak over the bay with childlike expectation, "Are they here?" I slowly scan the surface, hoping to catch the glistening of the first morning rays on dorsal fins. If dolphins are in, it is a quick wake up: I grab my fins and mask, eat a power bar, and run to the water, all the while intently observing their behavior – are they active or relaxed, awake or sleepy?

It's a good 10-minute swim out to where they like to hang out. I use that time to focus on my alignment. How do I feel, what are my thoughts, how is my energy flowing? And pay attention to my breathing, one of the easiest ways to come back into balance. I love hearing my breath through the snorkel, the sound makes it so easy to focus on.

There's something about the morning hours underwater. The visibility is exceptional. Everything is crisp and clear. The ocean teems with life. Coral, colorful fish, sea stars and occasionally an ancient turtle all remind me of the infinite beauty of nature. Swimming towards the middle of the bay, I observe how the seafloor changes. After a while, coral gives way to golden sands that seem to stretch into infinity in wave-like formations. As the depth increases, the color of the water becomes dream-like with beautiful shades of blue and golden sunrays piercing through. That's where I usually stop and take it all in; diving into this liquid heaven, I listen. Sometimes the clicks and whistles reach me before I see the dolphins. Sometimes I catch a glimpse of the pod coming from afar. Other times they sneak up on me from behind.

I don't think I'll ever get used to the beauty of a dolphin encounter. Be it a whole pod deep down below or a single, curious dolphin right next to me, a group of playful, vocalizing males or my favorite, a mom with a baby; I am always left speechless, in awe, filled with grace. Every encounter is personal, it reflects where I am and where the dolphins are, energetically. Always, it is a complex collage of feeling, intuition, thoughts, energy, and quantum understanding. But it is also as simple as just being; playing and enjoying each moment; dancing with what comes; breathing with my soul; receiving the gifts.

Every once in a while, there comes a day, when something extraordinary happens. It's impossible to predict ahead of time when it will happen. On these occasions, the whole pod emanates exuberance. The water is saturated with an energy of celebration. The dolphins spend time with you in such a profound way that it touches the very core of your being. You exit the water feeling blissful, stunned. Looking into the eyes of other swimmers as they come out, they confirm, "This was special!"

Three weeks after the choir, I experienced one of these once-in-a-lifetime moments. I was camping in the bay, ready for them, but dolphins hadn't shown up for a week. There was stillness in the air and the expectation was building. Then, on my last day in the bay, the pod showed up. It was around 7 a.m., and the excitement of seeing them rocketed me out of my sleeping bag. I was looking forward to singing the tones and sharing the beauty of our choir with them. But before I could sing a note, I was greeted with a pod that was oozing pure energy of joy and celebration!

I hardly even left the shore and started to swim, when I was met by two spinners that were coming towards me full speed, vocalizing and clicking like they were on a local radio station. I was laughing out loud as they reached me, turned around and swam back out. They were my escorts saying, "Come on, join the party!"

"What is going on?" was all I could think, hardly believing what I was seeing... They came out to only 30 feet away from the shore, to shallow waters, where I've never seen them before, just to do what: greet me?! "This is incredible." I mumbled to myself as I followed them out in the open. As I was swimming I remembered the tones and started singing tonal level 17, the dolphin tone, "Ha ha ha, ha ha ha" It was perfect, I felt how my cells started to dance and I knew the dolphins could hear me, so I was interested to see what would happen next.

I must admit, my memory of everything after that is kind of blurry. When I reached the middle of the bay and the entire pod approached me, it felt like I was pulled into their bubble of joy and that joy was so intense and overpowering, that now, looking back, it seems like a dream. It was probably the closest to heaven on Earth I've ever been. There were other people in the water, but I never saw them. I had close and intimate contact with dolphin after dolphin, they were all around me, spinning me, playing games, moms were bringing their babies right up to my face and letting us play together. Most important is the feeling I had, the ecstasy, the joy: simply indescribable. I may have been in another reality altogether, experiencing a glimpse into the future, into a higher state of awareness, receiving a gift from beyond.

I kept toning through the whole event and the spinners were responding, sometimes vocally, sometimes through their movement. It was amazing to share and communicate in a wordless, multidimensional manner. I was sending them mental pictures of the choir and our celebration of the shift and observing their response. It was spectacular, and I am forever grateful for what I received on that day.

I was sitting on the beach afterwards, watching swimmer after swimmer come out with the biggest smiles. I could tell they got it too. We were all blissed out. A good friend walked up to me and said, "I've been here for 20 years, swimming with them daily, and today was in the top 3 of my all-time favorites. It was absolutely out of this world!"

Aotearoa – The Land of the Long White Cloud (and Liveliest Dolphins!)

The 3 months I'd spent in Hawai'i were over too quickly, but my journey had just begun. I boarded a ten-hour, overnight plane to Aotearoa, New Zealand. We were landing in Auckland as the orange sunrise was coloring the clouds, and I noticed my heart well up with a sentimental feeling. This pristine land felt different and yet the same. It had a beautiful Lemurian, home-like energy, yet it felt more spread out, empty, and unexplored than Hawai'i. Kryon calls New Zealand the second Lemuria, he says when the landmass around Hawai'i started to sink, Lemurians took to their boats in hopes of finding a new home. The currents took them to South Pacific islands, Rapa Nui and Aotearoa.[6] They recreated their society in these new places with the same sacred energy and teachings. You can feel the loving embrace of Lemurian energy etched into the Crystalline grid of New Zealand.

It's never easy for me to leave Hawai'i, but this time the transition was made easier by spending my first week off the islands in a teepee in a remote, green valley near the city of Thames, swimming in a river and merging with the land. My journey then took me across North Island to a music festival in New Plymouth and through Wellington to the South Island which should be on the bucket list of every nature and Lord of the Rings movie fan. After a week, I found myself in a little town called Kaikoura. Reason: dusky dolphins. Intent: to tone and have fun!

"Sing to them, they love it when you sing to them." were the words of our tour guide, who was briefing us on the behavior of dusky dolphins before the tour. "Isn't that interesting?" I murmured to myself, as I was pulling on an inch-thick wetsuit that would supposedly shield me from the freezing cold waters of the South Island. "I wonder if he listens to Kryon?" I was surprised to see my latest discovery, toning to dolphins, so quickly confirmed and reflected in my reality!

It was early morning, and I was watching the first sun rays peak out from behind the majestic mountaintops of the Southern Alps, as our boat was cruising alongside the shore. The color of the water in New Zealand is a very distinct greenish hue. I believe it comes from the abundance of rivers bringing in mud and composted materials. I would soon learn it also creates rather poor underwater visibility.

Locating dolphins was extremely easy. All we had to do, was take our boat around the long peninsula that makes Kaikoura look so unique from the air. There they were, dusky dolphins on their morning break ("Coffee, anyone?"). I had to hold my breath. It wasn't a pod of ten or twenty. There were a few hundred of them! And they were far from serene. Lots of coming and going, lots of air acrobatics and I realized as I entered the water, there was lots of chit-chatting as well. But I couldn't see a thing! The beautiful green water made it hard to even see my fins. How was I going to find dolphins? No worries. They found me.

"Sing to them!" Those words were still echoing in my ears as I started to swim. So, I opened my mouth and allowed the tones to vibrate through the waters. Now, you would have thought that after all these years, I would be better prepared for a meeting, but nope, dolphins surprised me again.

The duskies were like balls of excitement zig-zagging through my energy field. I heard them all around me, but I couldn't see them coming. They suddenly showed up in huge numbers and with immense speed. They were everywhere. They were much smaller than spinner or bottlenose dolphins, and they moved erratically and unpredictably. It was like walking into a gym where kids are having recess – almost impossible for the five senses to take it all in.

Poor visibility makes dusky dolphins more dependent on sound as a way of interacting and communicating. That's why they love it when you join their choir and sing. Their curiosity then gives them no choice but to come and check you out.

At first, they just sped through my space, gently observing from a distance. But soon some of them started to slow down and stop in front of my face, looking into my eyes, clicking, whistling, and chirping.

And before I realized, they were playing with me, a game I started to call "Spinning OOMM." A dolphin hovered in front of my face, created eye-contact, and then started to swim around me in a circle. I wanted to keep up, so I had to start spinning. Dusky would love it and do another circle. I'd follow. And again. He started going faster and faster, spinning me "Out of My Mind" (OOMM). My toning, which until that moment had a serious vibe, gave way to laughter. I felt so silly and childlike! After a while all the whirling made me so dizzy I couldn't continue. Reading my thoughts, the dolphin simply swam away and allowed me to take a few deep breaths. After I had collected myself, another dusky joined me and started to spin me again. All day long. (Well, for the few hours when we were there, but you get my point). They loved it. And I loved it too! I couldn't remember the last time I'd laughed so hard. It was so child-like, playful, exciting. It felt like spinning emptied me out and turned off my logic, my left brain.

I later remembered Kryon mentioned that little kids spin naturally, all over the world, no matter what culture. He explained it has to do with magnetics – it helps to balance human's electro-magnetic field. And then there are whirling dervishes, who perform a dance called "Sema," to achieve the wisdom and love of God. Do dolphins innately "know" these things or are they just playing? Could it be that they somehow sense or see our electro-magnetic field and notice a change after the game? One thing is for sure: I saw a change in my co-swimmers. Dolphins spun everyone in our group. As I was walking home afterwards with a few of my traveling friends, everybody was different. We were like little kids, free of worries, laughing and dancing on the sidewalk.

Sailing Through South Pacific

I was soon to experience another level of how powerful dreaming, imagination and synchronicity are. I call it a multi-layered synchronicity, when gifts come on many levels, and wishes and intents, dreamt about for years, all get fulfilled in a single event, involving many people and places. For me that event was a 4-month sailing journey across South Pacific.

Since my first experience with dolphins, I've also felt an immense connection with whales. They visited me in my dreams frequently, I had their pictures on my wall and I kept on saying, "One day, I get to see you underwater, gentle giants." But even after all the snorkeling hours I'd logged with dolphins, I still wasn't sure how to go about meeting a whale underwater.

If I compare my early relationship with whales to dancing, I would say it was like being enchanted by a magnificent dancer on the other side of the room, but unsure of how to approach her. So, for us to come together she'd have to take the first step towards me. Right before I left Hawai'i, a humpback mom with her calf swam into the dolphin bay where I was camping. They came right into the middle of the bay, where spinners liked to hang out and have fun with us. The humpbacks stayed for a few minutes as everyone on the beach watched in awe. Some people swam out, but I knew I was supposed to just stand there and breathe in their energy. It was like an introduction, to open my field to what was to come.

After my time with dusky dolphins, I got a job in Arthur's Pass, a small village high up in the Southern Alps.

The beauty of nature there was breathtaking. I loved hiking through endless beech forests, alongside little streams, and waterfalls, immersing myself in the pure, crystalline energy of Gaia.

But then the snow storms arrived. We could get up to 2 feet of snow in one day. The roads would close and the whole world would immerse itself in winter stillness. I started to daydream a lot. I was traveling in my imagination, visiting golden beaches and lush green mountains of the South Pacific. I knew that Tonga, one of best places in the world to swim with humpback whales, was just a quick flight away. But I wanted to explore another option first – sailboats. When I was 18 a friend of mine took me on a week-long sailboat trip to Croatia. I loved it so much, I joked that we should steal a sailboat and sail around the world. That planted a seed that was now ready to germinate.

While the Alps were putting on their winter adornments, I was busy writing to different sailboats searching for crew. I knew it wouldn't be easy, people usually like to meet you in person when they are about to share a small boat with you for a few months, but after a couple of weeks I got a positive reply. Jimmy from Ireland, who was currently in Tahiti, would be happy to have me onboard for the next 4 months, traveling from

French Polynesia to Cook Islands and lastly, Tonga. Bingo!!!

Living on a boat was one of the most colorful and fulfilling experiences of my life. I loved waking up in the morning, expecting each day to be filled with adventures. It was magical when I could take a little dinghy and choose between snorkeling at the reef or finding a little inlet and exploring the land on foot. Being with the ocean was a grand gift and there was so much to learn. Whenever we left one island and approached another, I always felt that this was how traveling was supposed to be: gradually releasing the old, transitioning, then gradually discovering the new. Crossings could be challenging, sometimes it took days before we saw land again. But that time was like a very deep meditation.

There was only endless ocean, everywhere I looked. It was calling me deeper within, to dive into my darkest places. It was like experiencing the stillness of winter within my own being, especially on night watches. Every 3 hours another person would take the helm and watch for any ships or tankers in our way. The night sky was full of stars and it was impossible to tell where it merged with the ocean. I would sit there alone, in the dark, waves coming and going and the only thing that was reminding me of everyday reality were the instruments I had to check periodically – wind, boat speed, direction,

GPS, travel log. The veil that separates our world from other dimensions is thinner out on the ocean. It was easy to forget my physicality and let my soul just soar into the infinite darkness.

Seeing the land after days at sea was an experience that every cell felt and acknowledged. The smells, the sights, the sounds... everything was vibrant and colorful. And after we anchored, my main job was to explore! How exciting!

"I Am Coming with You!"

My first crossing was from Tahiti to Moorea, a little heart shaped island that carries a very strong energy. We anchored in Opunohu bay on the North side, in the most stunning turquoise water I had ever seen. We had a view of three sharp peaks across the bay (one of them looking like a needle) and my body was vibrating every time I looked at them. I spent hours just sitting and feeling the energy coming towards me, breathing, and receiving.

"What are you doing?" asked Francoise, a French lady, who was spending a week with us on the boat, deciding if she wanted to stay longer.

"I'm listening to the mountain. It's talking."

"What is it saying?"

I had no idea. All I knew was that my cells were vibrating, like a "hum" sound was coming from the mountain and pulsating in my body. But what was it saying??

The answer came a few days later. We hitched up a road that took us to a view point in the middle of the island. We came surprisingly close to the "needle peak" and as I was exploring a little plateau, taking in the views, I discovered a small trail in between the trees. It was heading towards the "singing mountain." I felt a strong desire to get as close to the peak as possible. Jimmy and Francoise joined me on the trail and after a couple of hours we came to a fork – one trail went down, back towards the bay and the other across the middle of the island, right under the needle. I wanted to take it, but there was only an hour of daylight left and I knew we had to start descending, or we would get lost in the jungle. But the call of the mountain was so strong, I just couldn't leave. Not yet.

I looked at my friends and said, "I'll catch up with you in a little bit, I need a minute by myself here." I sat down and closed my eyes. I could feel that same vibration that was coming towards me for days, only louder. I had a strong desire to merge with the mountain, to deeply immerse myself in her "hum." I didn't want to leave it behind. It felt so good to be in her presence, like I was being gently rocked in the womb of mother Earth. "I don't want to leave," I murmured, releasing a big sigh. And that's when I finally heard the mountain speak. She said, "I'm coming with you." To my surprise, I could see the mountain in my mind's eye, she got up and deliberately took a stand behind me, joining with my guides.

This was, yet again, one of those moments that stretched my understanding of reality. How is this possible? How can a mountain do that? Isn't it too big? When I share this, I like to invite people to feel into their multidimensional reality. If time and space don't exist on the other side, you can have a mountain walking right beside you, loving you. It's a reminder that we are much bigger than we think.

This was just the first in a line of amazing synchronicities that were part of my South Pacific journey. Almost every island I landed on, guided me to a sacred place, where an ancient energy was waiting to be witnessed and integrated. Pineal Tones were the key to this whole process. When I entered a sacred place, the tones started flowing out of my mouth, effortlessly, and then magic happened. The land knew me and expected me. There was a feeling of union and celebration, as I merged with the gifts contained within the rocks and dirt.

Now, looking back, I understand that I was collecting pieces of my Lemurian incarnations. Kryon tells us that most of us only had one lifetime in the original Lemuria. But when we moved we created societies with similar energy in our new homelands, the second Lemurias. My intuition tells me I've had dozens of lifetimes in this energy, on many of the islands I've visited (including Aotearoa). My journey allowed for the beauty, the truth and the sacredness of these incarnations to permeate my whole being, so now everywhere I walk, I carry the fullness of my Lemurian expression with me. I am Lemuri Jan, one and many.

Besides Moorea, there is another island that shook me to the core of my being – Rarotonga. Our boat was tied in a small harbor on the North side, in a town called Avarua. I gifted myself a day of exploring, hitch-hiking and visiting beaches.

"Where would be a good place to watch the sunset?" I asked a very friendly older guy, who picked me up hitching in the late afternoon.

"Black Rock Beach," was his reply.

He dropped me off at a gorgeous white sand beach with an amazing view. I dove into the lagoon and enjoyed the days last rays of sun. I looked at the black cliffs at the end of the beach and decided to walk towards them. Coming closer I realized a huge black boulder was separated from the cliff, standing by itself 20 feet out into the ocean. My inner child, who loves climbing, decided we were going to ascend to the top. I waded around the giant black rock, trying to find a good climbing route, when it suddenly hit me. This rock was sacred! Inside the walls were holes, creating mouths, eyes and noses. Numerous faces emerged, and I knew without a doubt, they were the faces of the ancestors!

Honoring the sacredness, I closed my eyes and asked for a permission to enter, singing "Aloha e" three times. The energy embraced me and invited me in. I made it to the top and found a little nook to sit in and soak up the warmth coming from the blackness of the rock. The sun just touched the horizon as I started to sing the tones. I closed my eyes and realized that ancestors were adding their energy to my song. They were singing with me! Time and space disappeared, and I was melding with multidimensional realities, within myself and within the rock. My heart filled with love and profound peace descended on me, as all the pieces clicked into their rightful place. I was back home!

The next day, my friend was reading Lonely Planet and as she came to the section about Black Rock Beach she read this sentence, "Black Rock (Turou), is traditionally believed to be where the spirits of the dead commenced their voyage to 'Avaiki (the afterworld)."

The Call of a Whale

With each passing day on the boat, I fell deeper in love with the ocean. I loved every color, every movement. The pure turquoise of the lagoons, the deep indigo of the open waters, the rolling of the big waves on the crossings, the breaking of the small curls on the marina surface, the beauty of the underwater worlds ... Each island had something special to offer. Moorea has sting rays and underwater statues; Bora Bora has manta rays and colorful fish; Palmerston Atoll has turtles and pristine coral reefs; and Niue, sea snakes. I'd never felt so alive and so blessed.

But nothing can compare to the magnificence of one animal – the humpback whale. Meeting them underwater is so powerful, so majestic that however ready you think you are, you'll still be absolutely blown away. I think I subconsciously felt the immensity of what was coming, and the whales gifted me with a gradual introduction to their energy. We first saw them from afar, their white spouts in the distance, while crossing from French Polynesia to the Cook Islands. Then we headed to Palmerston Atoll, a tiny ring of small motus (reef islands) around the most lively and clear lagoon I've ever seen.

The passage through the reef wasn't big enough for a sailboat so we had to tie to a mooring in front of it. The locals then picked us up and introduced their time-forgotten world to us. Only 70 people lived on the island and they were all descendants of one man who had moved there with three wives a hundred years ago. Their only contact with the outside world was a cargo boat twice a year. Even though I enjoyed spending time with them, my fascination lay where our boat was. While snorkeling around it, I realized we were tied to an underwater shelf, that soon gave way to a deep channel, that seemingly stretched into infinity. And that's where, a few times a day, humpback whales came up for air. It was hardly more than 100 feet from our boat!

The problem was I could never predict when the whales would be there. It could be hours in between their visits, so we had to just go on with our lives, preparing meals, drinking tea, and enjoying ourselves at the cockpit table. And then, "Pfuussshhhhh!" The power of their exhale rocketed us from our seats. It was so splendid to witness them so close. In the night, when all the other sounds died off, it seemed they surfaced right next to our boat. They would usually take three deep breaths and then dive back down. They never stayed for more than a minute. One day, after exploring at the reef, I was climbing back on the boat, removing my fins, when I heard a spout.

"It's now or never!" I jumped back in and started swimming towards the whale. My feelings were mixed. I was both excited and a little scared – I was all alone in the deep blue, about to meet with one of the biggest animals on the planet. I was swimming with a steady rhythm and by the time I neared the edge of the underwater shelf, I could hear the last, third breath of the humpback and observed a huge, dark shadow slowly dive into the channel.

Thus, my first meeting with a gentle giant invited me to start breathing their energy deeper into my being. I was starting to feel all right (or so I thought) with how big they were. On the next island, Niue, they came within a few hundred yards of the coral reef where I enjoyed spending time with underwater snakes. I observed the whales from the beach and traveled out to them with my energy, breathing some more.

Then we got to Tonga. Vava'u is the northern most group of islands and to get to the marina, you need to sail in between many small islands and motus, almost like you're on a river. As we turned the corner on one of those, the channel in front of us opened wider, probably a few miles across. Right in the middle of it was a mother whale with a baby, lying on the water, just waiting for us (or so it seemed). We got into two dinghies and slowly approached them. They dove down and disappeared for a few minutes. I thought we would see them resurface somewhere far away, so I was checking the horizon, when a loud spout brought me back. They came up for air right in between our two little dinghies!

We jumped in and swam towards them, and my longtime dream was fulfilled! Humpbacks allowed us to approach them and then they slowly swam past us (moms tail went up and down barely 6 feet away from me!) as they gently dove down into the depths, disappearing from sight. I was ecstatic! It felt like puzzle pieces that were floating in my energy field, suddenly clicked into their rightful place. In that moment, I was at peace with death. I hope everyone gets to experience this kind of fulfillment at least once in their lives. It is moments like this that make the Earth experience so worthy and magical. I call them "the moments of eternity."

It was a few days later when I realized I wasn't done. Dreams were fulfilled, yes, but I felt there was more. I desired a deeper dance with the whales. I wanted to look into their eyes. I came so far to be with them and I wasn't just going to leave without trying to see them again. When I called into the whale-watching agency, they said the season was almost over and whales were slowly departing on their journey to Antarctica. They were also completely booked... I didn't give up. With the help of a local friend, I got a seat on one of the last boat tours heading out to see them.

The Magnificent Dance

"You may want to change your mind." said the captain to our little group, who had gathered at 7am on a pier. "We haven't seen a single whale in a week now. I'm hoping they haven't all left. We don't do returns on the money after the trip, whales or no whales."

I hesitated for a moment, lost in thoughts. I'd spent my last $300 on this tour and he was saying it might be all for nothing? I saw whales already, should I save my money for something else?

"No way!" The answer came from deep inside. I didn't sail across South Pacific, experiencing gift after gift, to now back off just because of money. "I am here, trusting in synchronicity. Whatever is meant to happen, will happen!"

A few minutes later we were motoring through the maze of little channels and islands of Vava'u. Tonga has a unique look, different than any other South Pacific island I've been to. Most of the main island is overgrown with jungle-like forests that reach all the way down to the water. The water in the channels is deep and whales love hanging out there, so you never know where you might stumble upon them.

"Ok, let's try our luck all the way at the outer islands," said the captain, after an hour of no success. As we traveled further, I noticed how the vegetation changed and was replaced with palm trees and golden sands, the kind that make deserted outer islands look so picture-perfect.

Everybody on the boat was immersed in their thoughts, wanting to see whales, but slowly losing hope. I observed how pessimistic thoughts gradually started to descend on me as well, but then something stirred in me and I shook off the melancholy. I started to tone, very quietly, just for myself, "Ah-ee-oh, ah-ee-oh" It felt good and it brought me back into alignment. It filled me with gratitude for the whole journey, for the most amazing 4 months of my life. I loved how The Journey of the Tones took me from one island to another, from one magical experience to the next. Then I decided I would sing to the whales, whether they were there or not. I closed my eyes and, in my imagination, observed humpbacks underwater. One turned towards me and that's when the captain's call brought me back, "There, I've seen something"

Everybody looked. A few minutes passed. Nothing. We started to move in that direction and I continued with toning. I noticed a white splash in the distance, but I couldn't tell if it was a whale or a wave. The captain dispersed my doubts, "It's definitely a whale, folks, keep your eyes open, we'll try to get closer." In a little bit the whale came up again, first a big spout and then a smaller one next to it – a mom and a baby! "We're lucky, get ready to go in," said the captain.

Fins, snorkels, cameras, excitement. We entered the water and witnessed two shadows in the distance, slowly moving on. "First time is usually like this, they just check you out from afar," explained Billy, a local tour guide who was there to assist us with snorkeling.

Our boat slowly moved alongside the whales and soon it was time to enter again. The humpbacks were right beneath us, but so far down, they looked like tiny fish, only an inch long. They were just staying there, motionless. My heart opened and out came the tones, "Ah-ee-oh, ah-ee-oh" I sounded funny through the snorkel, but I didn't care. What happened next was amazing.

The moment I started to sing, that same instant, the whales moved and began ascending. Did they hear me, feel me? I watched them coming closer and closer, starting to realize how big they were. I was breathing in their energy and as they approached, I felt I could burst if I took another breath. Mom was too big! And just like she knew what I was feeling, she stopped, 30 feet below us, allowing the baby to gracefully dance all the way up. My voice was shaking as it neared us and looked us in the eye, got some air, turned around and dove back to mom. Wow. That was so beautiful. Such gentleness, such grace.

The next time we went in, the whales once more looked like two dark specks, deep down below. It's hard to explain what happened next, I lost all rational control. My chest opened with an infusion of soft, gentle, loving energy, that moved my mouth and out came a whale sound – a high-pitched, long, almost lonely sounding tune, like a call for a lost family member. The whales stirred, like somebody woke them up from a nap, and started rising towards us. This time though, mom did something special.

She picked the baby up from underneath and put it on her nose. Then she slowly brought it up to us. At one point, baby rolled off her nose and spun in front of us, in the most graceful, fairy-like manner. It took a few breaths and stayed with us for a while. It made sure to look everyone in the eye and then dove back to mom. They slowly swam underneath us allowing us to keep up with them for a while. I was moved beyond tears. There was something so profoundly tender and timeless in the way mom picked up her baby. I was sobbing from pure beauty, something moved me on a very deep, ancient level. It felt like eternity manifested itself in front of my eyes in pure perfection. As I was climbing back on the boat, I realized their dance left me totally speechless, shaken... their majestic presence changed me, forever.

Sitting there, I was wondering how I could possibly receive anything else. When you travel to the heart of the Universe, how can you open to even more? I had no idea, but the baby whale did. It was time to play!

As we swam with them for the last time, baby whale turned into a real kiddo! It started to splash and create thousands of bubbles. It got us all giggling, especially after hiding behind the bubbles and then sneaking up on us, from behind. So much fun! I didn't expect tricks like this from a whale, but, hey, he was only a baby after all. I'm sure his mama was saying, “Be nice to humans, ok? They are so small, you can't just bump into them.” The play continued as we motored back to the marina, traveling alongside the whales, the baby breached and jumped countless times, just for fun. We all clapped, cheered, and laughed. What a way to finish the day. And for the grand finale, mom breached two times, the second time her whole body out of the water. OMG. Stunning. The gift of a lifetime!

In the days that followed, I couldn't really speak to people. I sat on the beach for hours, just breathing and watching the ocean, tears flowing down my cheeks. I felt the whales were calling from the depths of my being, inviting me to embody their vulnerability, gentleness, and grace. To bring in their playfulness, ease, and joy. Breath after breath. Breath after breath.

Shasta – Beginning of A New Life

Have you ever had a plan and just when it seemed like it was working out, suddenly everything shifted so dramatically that you needed to throw your plan away and go on a road trip?

That's what happened to me the next year in Mt. Shasta. I showed up thinking I knew what was going on. I was to sing the tones as a part of the third Lemurian choir, to activate the time capsule within the node of Shasta (I will explain that in a second). I ended up getting married and becoming a father to a beautiful soul, who was, believe it or not, waiting for us inside the mountain. Oh yes, and it all happened on a road trip. So, what did I learn from this? To expect the unexpected. Or better yet to use Kryon's words, "Unexpected benevolent change." Yup, that about summarizes it!

So how did this come about? After I returned to New Zealand to integrate my South Pacific journey, I was soon presented with a new piece of information that got me really excited about the future: the time capsules of the planet. Kryon explained what the Maui choir really did. "Turning the key in the lock" was a metaphor for a system of time capsules within nodes and nulls, that were left for humanity on the grids of the planet, and were now ready to be activated.

Monika Muranyi talks in-depth about time capsules, nodes and nulls in a beautiful summary posted on her website, that I highly encourage you to read and get the broader picture.[7] Here's a short few lines from Monika,

"Long ago the Pleiadians looked at this planet and they selected 12 pairs of energy points. They would represent the duality of the planet. These 12 pairs are found at 24 geographical locations. A total of 24 nodes and nulls, on mountain peaks and in deserts, were selected as the most promising places on the planet. Kryon has called these 12 polarized node and null energy pairs, time capsules. Energy was set in these places so that if humanity should ever make it to a higher consciousness these places would release information for the individual Human Being as well as for the whole planet."

I will reveal how time capsules are connected to cetaceans in the next chapter. Here, the big piece of the puzzle is that the Lemurian choir, when singing the Pineal Tones to the nodes and nulls, has an ability to activate and calibrate the time capsules, thereby releasing the information onto the grids of the planet. This then allows anyone to pick it up: scientists can come up with new inventions, philosophers with new ideas, and humanity in general can tune into a more compassionate, loving energy that is planting the seeds for peace on Earth.

So, the choir in Maui was just the beginning. In years to come the choir would gather in places like the Yucatan peninsula in Mexico, Mt. Shasta in California, Uluru in Australia, the ancient land of Israel, and Mt. Ida, a quartz crystal mecca in Arkansas.

I was too late to catch the Yucatan choir but could save some money and make it to Mt. Shasta. On my way to the mountain, there was a surprise waiting for me. I will call it Sacred Spinner Geometry. From New Zealand I flew to Hawai'i to spend some time with my dear dolphins. While excitedly sharing with them one of the new Pineal tones that I had learned for the Shasta choir, they circled me in beautiful patterns of sacred geometry. They approached me in pairs and swam around me in ways I'd never seen before. A couple would circle right in front of my eyes, while another pair made circles deep down beneath me, moving in both clock-wise and counter-clockwise directions! They extensively clicked and whistled in harmony with my toning, and it felt like we were communicating through sound (similar to echoing pairs of our toning choir), and pattern.

Then it dawned on me: They were showing me the energy of the tones through their movement and sounds. I realized we were all contained within the multidimensional field of the toning level 25 that I was singing. We were creating a portal, receiving quantum energy and swimming within it. It was sacred geometry at its best!

Falling in Love

After traveling for a few years, I had become used to following my excitement. I always chose my next destination by what my intuition was telling me. My excitement for Shasta was so huge that I did something I otherwise never do: I booked my accommodations 4 months in advance! The go-with-the-flow, gypsy part of me thought this was nuts!

But something started to bother me as I came closer to Mt. Shasta. There were absolutely no signs as what to do after the choir. Blank space, no energy, like life after Shasta didn't exist. And to make it more complicated, my money was starting to run out!

I tried to make plans, but nothing worked. I talked to my guides and there was silence. What was going on?? My guides didn't say anything because they knew that if they'd said, "All is well. You will meet the love of your life, get married in a month and have a child a year later." I would have run the other way!

I can hear some of you saying, "Hey, wait a minute, what happened to your girlfriend that you left behind in Slovenia?" Well, soon after I left, she fell in love with another guy. And while that was really hard and required lots of breathing and releasing, it turned out to be a huge blessing on my path – I was now free to continue with my journey, for she was the only reason why I would ever have considered going back. But Shasta and the beautiful beings inside the mountain had other plans for me.

If you haven't heard anything about Mt. Shasta, this sacred mountain has been connected to many stories about an underground society that lives in a city of light called Telos. Probably the purest source of information are books by Aurelia Jones, who channeled a high priest from Telos, named Adama.[8] He explained that Telosians are Lemurians who moved there after their continent sank and built a city within the mountain that is slightly more quantum than our physical reality. According to Adama they are waiting for humanity's spiritual awakening to signal the right moment for them to merge with us on the surface again.

The Lemurian choir gathered in Mt. Shasta to sing the Pineal tones to a node in the mountain that is connected to a Lemurian underground city. As we sang the tones, activating and calibrating the node that is Mt. Shasta, the feeling of celebration was palpable. At one moment, I closed my eyes, and traveled to the city in the mountain, and what I saw was astounding: the Lemurians were singing back to us! Their song was multidimensional – beautiful colors and laughter were woven into the sounds. It was mesmerizing.

Their song also contained a deep honoring that made me well up. Lemurians were thanking us and celebrating what we were doing. And then a new clarity emerged. Many of the things Aurelia talked about, should be viewed as metaphors and understood as part of the system of nodes and nulls. It is the wisdom of our Lemurian and Star Akash that is awakening within us and that is why the time capsules are opening. It is not for us to wait for Lemurians to come out of the mountain, but instead to claim that energy within us and walk this planet as compassionate, multidimensional humans!

I became friends with one of the attendees, a beautiful woman named Kirsten on Facebook prior to the event. I had no idea she was my wife-to-be! We talked online as I was traveling and decided to meet in person and camp on the mountain the night before the choir. I was in love with her as soon as I saw her. My wife has an appearance of a fairy, whenever I look at her I feel lightness in my heart and I have to smile. It is so easy to get lost in her eyes, looking into the depths of her magnificent soul. Meeting her on Mt. Shasta felt like coming home. I wanted to be in her presence all the time.

We could talk till 4am every night and then attend the events in the day-time. I felt no tiredness, I was flying high with the love I could feel in every cell of my being. She was the woman from my past, that my healer friend James had talked about, the woman I fell in love with in the British Isles. James helped me release her and anything lingering from that lifetime, only to have Universe bring her back to me two years later!

After the choir, we traveled through Redwood forests to her home in Oregon, and on the way decided we wanted to stay together, but because I was a foreigner, I would have to leave the country soon – wouldn't it be easier just to get married? And so we did.

We didn't know at the time, that coming with us from Shasta, was a special, beautiful being, who was to be our child. We would soon learn. Every time we made love, the room would fill with a presence, it felt like hundreds of souls were there watching us. It was surreal, and we knew what it meant.

"Stay away." We talked to the "empty" space around us. "We need some time to just be together and get to know one another. We want to travel and enjoy life. Give us a couple of years!" They didn't listen. It seemed like our will was overpowered, but we knew better. On a soul level, we agreed.

Our higher selves made sure we understood the appropriateness of this conception, so we received many confirmations throughout pregnancy. Probably the biggest one, was a vision I saw while we were breathing with the incoming soul.

We did something special, called Dreamwalker Birthing, where you take time every night to breathe and open your consciousness, to reach through the dimensions and connect with the soul coming to be your child. In one of those sessions, I was taken out of my body and had a vision. I saw myself and Kirsten in a little meadow on the slopes of Mount Shasta. It was dark, but the moonlight was bright enough for us to see each other. We left our car running, on the road, with lights turned on. We walked a few hundred feet through the forest to reach this clearing, a little meadow where we were now standing. In front of us was a being in spirit form, emanating a beautiful, sacred, peaceful light. It was floating about three feet off the ground and I had an innate feeling that this being was both from the stars and inside the mountain.

The interesting part, was that my vision lasted only one second, but everything I just described was known to me in that single second. And the next thing that happened was all three of us, Kirsten, me and the beautiful star being, while looking at each other, said out loud, "Yes!" and I was back in my body, in our room, breathing with Kirsten. I knew without a doubt that our "Yes!" was an agreement, for this being to become our child. It was also a confirmation that my higher self consciously chose every single thing that happened on that mountain – and knew it would be just too much for my human self to know these things in advance. That's why there was silence, emptiness, no clear potentials. I now celebrate it as the biggest gift of my life. The gift of Mt. Shasta!

Mt. Ida – The Dolphin Node

Every choir is special. There simply is not enough space here to share what happened on other nodes (maybe in another book), but I have to conclude this chapter with the Crystalline choir in Mt. Ida and the "dolphin synchronicity". It is the node that is closely related to this book and everything I'm talking about. Event after event, synchronicity after synchronicity, led me to the bigger picture of Mt. Ida's connection to the cetaceans.

"You need to come with me. I've discovered something amazing. I can hear whales singing when I dive into the crystalline lake!" Carol was excitedly sharing her experience knowing about my love for dolphins. She was a local woman who had just stopped by when we had our volunteer meeting the day before the choir started. Love for crystals brought her to Arkansas 26 years before and she never left. She had a small boat, on a lake that has a bottom made of giant crystals. When taking the boat out and diving into the water one day, she clearly heard the sounds of humpbacks calling from far away. She wanted me to come with her and experience it myself.

Arkansas was hot and humid. It was the thick of summer and swimming in a lake sounded like a great idea. Swimming while immersing myself in a whale song? Even better! As our boat took off, I loved watching the shoreline and feeling the energies of the crystalline lake. After half an hour, it was time to dive in. It felt so good to allow the water to wash off the sweat and cool me down. Even though the water was clear I couldn't see the bottom and as I dove down I was embraced by dark green color stretching in every direction. But I couldn't hear a thing. What was Carol hearing? Could it be that she was tapping into a multidimensional energy of a whale song? Or was the song somehow contained in the crystals and her love for them allowed her to hear it?

I had no idea, but my questions would soon be answered. What I didn't understand then was that Carol's story was just the first piece of a puzzle. As soon as the choir started, new revelations came in. I closed my eyes to take a few deep breaths and align before the event. In my mind's eye, I could clearly see three dolphin beings in their light bodies, and they were standing upright, like humans.

It felt like they were sent as some kind of emissaries, with a message to deliver. I smiled and greeted them, and they said, "When you sing the tones today, sing them for us as well. We will merge with your voice to add our song to the choir."

Next Kahuna Kalei, a Hawaiian priestess, came on stage to perform a sacred chant and invite in the ancestors. Then she felt inspired to speak a few words, and she shared that she felt a strong presence of dolphins and whales in the room. How's that for a synchronicity? There's more.

Kryon channeled between different segments of the tones, like he always does with the choir. He took the word "CRYSTAL," and gave a short message connected to each of the letters in the word. Letter "S" stood for "singing," and Kryon told us the Earth was singing to us, and then invited us to feel a song coming from the crystal mountain underneath us. I was sitting there, thinking about Carol and the song of the whales. She heard the node! But Kryon wasn't done.

One thing that happens as the node is activated and calibrated, is it then gets matched with a null. Kryon revealed that this node matched with Mt. Fitzroy in Patagonia, where whales come in large numbers to have babies!

Here are his words, "Whales are the living Crystalline grid. They are the ones that carry the Crystalline grid into the oceans. They are the library of consciousness for this planet. You've known this, you had to know this, you have cherished them, you have laughed when they jumped out of the water. You've looked them in the eye, you've felt their wisdom. Every country in the world, if they have any kind of sense, they would have an agreement not to kill this animal, and many of them do. This is revered, the humanity of the Earth is starting to recognize the value of this animal.

It is a multidimensional thing that they have, they carry what the planet cannot in the Crystalline grid, the living Crystalline grid. And you seek them out, Doctor [Dr.Todd], you make their noises and you want to sing to them, you want to even hang upside down in the water to emulate what they do. And this is why. Therefore, I will tell you that the null associated with the node that is crystalline, is Mt. Fitzroy in Patagonia. Doesn't it make sense – that's where the whales are ... the place that they go to to make and have children is important, because the children then receive the Crystalline information. The very activation that you're making today goes right to them through Mt. Fitzroy."[9]

What an amazing experience! Every bit of information merged in a beautiful overview. Carol was indeed right. The node was singing to her and she could hear the whales within that song coming through a null all the way from Patagonia!

But even that wasn't the full picture yet. There was a little hidden gem that only I could discover. It was a little detail that was hiding in plain sight, all that time. It dawned on me a few months later, when I was working on my website and a friend of mine mentioned, "InnerDolphinAwakening.com might be too long, how about an acronym, have you tried seeing if ida.com is available?" It wasn't. But then I saw it, IDA.com ... Mt. IDA!!! The mountain of Inner Dolphin Awakening!!!

Exercise 4: Discovering Your Soul Song

While I highly recommend learning the tones in a weekend workshop, it is not hard to start exploring on your own. Toning can be practiced by anyone, doesn't matter if you have music talent or not. The most known form of toning is singing, "OM," in yoga groups. The best way to start experiencing the benefits of toning is to take the basic 5 vowels: A, E, I, O, U and spending an extended time with each one of them. Take a deep breath and just sing the same vowel again and again, observing its effects inside your body and energy field.

Then start exploring the relationships between vowels. Travel from one to another, taking time to explore the little spaces in between. You can also play with exploring the relationships between vowels and certain consonants like: M, N, S and Z.

My soul song came to me after an hour of toning. I was sitting next to a stream in a forest in Southern Australia. I was just playing with different sounds when my toning suddenly shifted and out came a beautiful tune, one that filled my being with lightness and joy. I knew I'd discovered my soul song.

I hereby invite you to do the same. Could it be that your intent alone can bring out your unique song? Just explore and have fun!

• CHAPTER 6 •

Explanations and Explorations

WHAT IS TELEPATHY?" "Can I really speak with dolphins?" "Do I have a dolphin inside as well?" "How can I connect with it?"

This chapter tries to answer some of these questions. Over the years I have had plethora of insights, some through my guidance and intuition, and others from outside sources that I've resonated with. We are all unique and it is important for you to follow your intuition as we navigate through the following explanations. All I ask, as you read this chapter (and anything else in this book, really) is to stay with that gentle whisper of knowing that comes from your soul. Stay with what resonates and expand your understanding only when it feels right to you... that said, do have fun exploring with me! I honor you and I appreciate your uniqueness. And so it begins.

Unexpected Twist

I thought I had a very good idea about how this chapter was going to look. Until I started to write it. For days I kept on trying and nothing really flowed. I was correcting words and sentences frequently and kept on starting anew. This was nothing like the rest of the book, which was written in a joyful and effortless manner, with a smile on my face. Why was I struggling? And then one day, to top it all off, everything that was written in this chapter disappeared overnight. I opened the file and it was empty.

A psychic friend, who was visiting with me at the time, said, "You know, you'll be channeling dolphins and other beings?" Why would that be, I thought to myself. I knew for one, if I tuned into dolphin energy, their message would be very short, "Be joyful!" So, I didn't even bother to try.

But then I woke up at 3am one morning and couldn't fall back asleep. I decided to start writing, not minding the early hour. Before I could type my first word, I felt a presence enter my energy field and lay on my chest, almost like trying to put itself between me and the computer. My mind was completely empty, I couldn't for the life of me remember what this chapter was going to be about. Instead of forcing the issue, I decided to allow the energy on my chest to express itself through my words. Here's what came out,

"And now dear human, we come to the next chapter. We dolphins, are taking a more active role in taking this teaching further. This gentle soul Jan, has done a pretty good job, don't you think? We love him dearly. Take a deep breath. Do you believe dolphins can speak to you?

Don't judge us by our words, but by the energy presented. If we really are your cousins, your sea brothers, we are going to have feelings for you, family with family. We will have messages of love and encouragement. We will know what's going on inside you, and we will love you for it.

You are in the right place, dear human. Blessed be your soul that brought you to this point. We love you dearly. Come, join us now, swim in the ocean with us. Open your imagination and join us in the warm waters, that gently touch your skin, and remind you of the pure bliss of your multidimensional state. Did you know your womb is made of ocean, to help you transition from your soul-state into your human-state?

Every time you swim in the ocean you help yourself remember a little of what is on the other side. Your body relaxes, and your mind lets go. Suddenly, you see the beauty and you understand there's more to life than being stressed about what's not there. In flows the remembrance of how well you really are, just as you are. Ahhh. So good. Can you feel that right now?

And now imagine us, how we join you in the waters, your sea brothers. We are beautiful beings of light and joy. And we say to you, 'You have the same light inside. Come find it. Come breathe it in. Come play with us.' And you smile.

Can it be so simple? Can the truth just come to you? Don't you have to work hard to get it? Not at all. We are here to tell you: It is easy. Just look at us. We are not working at it. We are not going to school for it. There are no mystery schools where we're from. Only joy.

Could it be that your being is only joy? Could it be that your consciousness, really, is having fun being in all these different bodies and timelines and dimensions? How would that feel?

It feels good, doesn't it? Can you breathe with that and let everything else go? Can you come back to yourself?

We love you dearly and swim within your being forever. For we are you. There's a dolphin inside you and your magnificence wouldn't be the same without it. It is our pleasure to be of service. It is our joy to see you as you are: a beautiful being of light. Now, isn't it time you see it for yourself?

Yes.

And the circle is complete.

Blessings, the dolphins"

Our Multidimensional Nature

We are multidimensional beings. It is hard for the mind, which is so often caught up in the physical world, to grasp the concept of multidimensionality, to comprehend a world that is not limited by time and space, a world with a soul that is one and many. That is why the use of metaphor is helpful.

Imagine a beautiful flower, that has petals of vibrant colors and different shapes. Each petal has a unique signature, its own color and a specific vibration. It is almost like a song, a constant harmonious resonance that is being broadcast in all directions. As you tune into each song, you realize, they all sing of love.

This is what I call the flower of the soul, a representation of our multidimensional nature. Each flower petal represents a piece of our soul, that is unique in its vibration but always tied into the whole. For me this realization came as an experience in a meditation, where I could see silhouettes around me and recognized them as my guides. Each guide stepped forward and shared its essence with me, a specific color, and a unique vibration of love. When they were done, I had a vision of a grand flower, and together with my guides became the colorful petals. In the middle was the I AM, the higher self. When a flower says, "I AM," it exists through every aspect of itself, it exists as many flavors of love. When the human petal remembers it is a part of the flower, other petals are revealed, one by one. Our magnificence lives in many places and is inviting you to recognize and integrate it.

The experience of morphing into a dolphin, that I described in the beginning of the book, was my first physical experience of my multidimensionality. The moment I became a dolphin, I experienced myself as both human and dolphin. It was the most natural sensation, I had absolutely no problem being in two bodies at the same time. I believe my inner dolphin is one of the petals on the flower of my soul. It is no more or less important than other petals, but it brings in its own unique, beautiful, joyful essence. I believe everybody has an inner dolphin. When we experience "dolphin bliss," after a swim in the ocean with cetaceans, we actually experience a piece of our multidimensional nature and through it we connect to our soul.

In 2014, after I already started to dream this book into existence, I attended Kryon's meeting in Portland, where Lee Carroll, the channel for Kryon, presented a slide of "9 Attributes of The Soul" and guess what? Kryon was speaking about the same thing! Although he was supposedly very secretive and didn't want to say too much about it, so Lee Carroll put a big question mark next to "Cetaceans" on the slide. I wanted to get up and say, "I'm writing a book about it!" I didn't do it, but now, 3 years later, I am finally publicly answering what that question mark was about (from my perspective at least, I'm sure there's more).

According to Kryon, the human soul has 9 attributes. He organizes them in groups of three: Human group ((1) Higher Self, (2) Innate, (3) Human Consciousness), Angelic group ((4) Higher Self, (5) Soul Split, (6) Guides) and Support/Gaia group ((7) Higher Self, (8) Crystalline, (9) Cetaceans).[1]

Just as you can't look only at one flower petal, to comprehend the beauty of the flower, you may wish to listen to Kryon's explanation in its entirety.[1] Also, to really dive deeper into the subject, there is a book that Monika Muranyi wrote based on this channel, called Human Soul Revealed, which I highly recommend.[2]

It strikes me as important that Cetaceans are the 9th attribute. Numerologically, number 9 represents completion. So, you could say, human soul is not complete without the cetaceans.

Re-uniting with your soul

Are dolphins part of you, or is your soul embodied in cetaceans somehow?

My answer is, "Both!" (short answer that will take the rest of the book to explain).

I believe throughout human history we mostly were-n't ready to claim and carry the magnificence of our being. So, we put it in many places. We left some parts on the other side. We projected our sacredness into guides, angels and masters. We left some of it as part of the earth, or better say the Crystalline grid. And we made a special agreement with cetaceans. We asked them to carry a part of our being until we were ready claim it. And my dear human, now is the time.

I didn't see the pattern at first, but over the years I've been asked by different energies if I was ready to take back my sacredness. When I first started doing Reiki, I practiced by doing sessions for friends and family. One of my friends had a bad knee injury from skiing. While I worked on him, I could sense and see the spirit of Mother Mary show up and what she did was kind of unusual. She stepped into me and merged her hands with mine, flowing her energy into my friend's knee. He turned to me a few minutes later, with a very bewildered look, "The pain is gone. My knee feels better."

I didn't understand what happened until Mother Mary came back many years later. I was meditating, and she showed up in front of my third eye, just looking at me. Then she stepped into me and simply merged with me. I sat there, waiting to see if she would do something else, when her message emerged in my mind, "I am not going anywhere, because I am you."

How do you explain that? I believe mother Mary represents my "divine feminine" petal that I projected onto her. She made sure I understood she was a part of me, one of the petals on my soul-flower. I am not saying Mother Mary might not be a separate being and it doesn't even matter. My point is that I asked her, probably in another lifetime, to carry a part of my divinity and now I'm integrating it back into myself.

Another event that had me reclaiming my divinity happened on Kauai, just a few years ago. I was sitting on the beach with my wife, breathing with the soul that was coming in as our child. Instead of connecting with the soul, I saw the ancient mountains of Kauai open and out came ancestors, by the thousands. They stood as one group above the ocean and a person in front, who was holding a beautiful golden bowl, full of pure, shining light, said to me, "We've been holding your divinity for eons. It is now time for you to take it back." I was sitting there, just breathing and receiving the immense energy of sacredness. To this day I am still taking in everything that was offered on that day.

And now we come back to dolphins and whales. What do you feel when you think about them? Do you feel joy, peace, love, or playfulness? Maybe, you're even one of those who experience what is called "the dolphin bliss?" Could it be, that cetaceans, just like the masters and ancestors, have something for you? Indeed, they do! Welcome to an awakening that has always been yours! Welcome to a reunion with a part of your soul!

Do you remember the metaphor of a dolphin/whale rider? In the story, the captain Arion jumped off his ship and was saved by riding a dolphin to the shore. Similarly, Paikea's canoe turned over and he was brought to Aotearoa on the back of a whale. Could it be that an awakening to one's quantum nature, is like a leap of faith, jumping into the ocean of the unknown (multidimensional reality)? What if, as you start swimming, you find out, just like Arion and Paikea did, that there's help, that takes you to the shore? In other words, when you truly embrace your inner dolphin, you'll be able to ride the energy of joy to a new life, embodying the magnificence of who you are. This energy will come from inside you, from your cells and your multidimensional soul. It's always been there, waiting for you to accept and integrate it. Your soul is not complete without the energy of joy, embodied in cetaceans of the planet.

We Came from The Stars

Exploring the nature of multidimensionality, I came to ask myself the question, "Could it be, that one of the flower petals of our multidimensional souls is an enlightened version of ourselves from another star system?" Here is my truth: Right beside each of us walks a Pleiadian, Sirian, Arcturian and many others. I believe the moment of enlightenment is the moment of complete melding of the petals of the flower with the Higher Self that is in the center. When that happens, that incarnation embodies all the attributes of the soul, and is not limited by time and space anymore. It can travel anywhere in the past, present or future, and becomes a guide to our other incarnations.

According to Kryon, planet Earth is the last in a line of planets to have gone through the test of duality, planets of free choice, between light and dark.[3] What does that mean? Free choice means that beings of divine origin can decide in each moment whether or not to align their thoughts and actions with the sacredness inside, individually and collectively. Societies go through cycles of light and dark until they come to a decision point – either to destroy themselves or wake up to the Creator inside. If they choose waking up, their vibration slowly increases over many millennia, until the collective consciousness reaches what we call enlightenment – a fully embodied remembrance of their multidimensionality.

If our souls are eternal, we must have had many lifetimes on other planets, and thus we experienced enlightenment many times before!

So, back to the question I asked above, "Could it be, that one of the flower petals of our multidimensional souls is an enlightened version of ourselves from another star system?"

Can you feel a presence around you, loving you, as you read these words? Are you ready yet to take a hand of your star sisters and brothers from different star systems, who all carry the same name in light as you do? When you open to their love, you begin to utilize the biggest support system – your multidimensional nature. And remember, if time and space don't matter, the enlightened you might even come from the future!

I hope this understanding makes it less strange when I say Pleiadians actually helped to start humanity. Lee Carroll, the channel for Kryon, said he was hesitant to share Kryon's message about our origins at first – it seemed too weird – so he found himself, synchronistically, talking to wise men of many ancient tribes all over the planet, and they told him the same thing, "We came from the stars."

I had the honor of talking to a Native American person while writing this book. I think I spoke to his heart when I sincerely thanked him for keeping their land closed off to anyone but their tribe. I feel it preserves the sacredness imbued in the land. When I shared this with him, he opened up to me. So, I decided to do what Lee Carroll does. I asked him, "What's your creation story? Where are we from?" He sighed, looked deeply into my eyes, not sure if I was ready to hear it or not. Then he decided to speak out and he said two simple things, "We are not from here." He pointed up to the sky. "We came from there."

Here is my summary of Kryon's creation story: The last planet of free choice before Gaia, was in the star system of Pleiadies. They went through their decision point and woke up to Creator inside. Over the thousands of years that followed, they came to such high vibration and enlightenment, that they became almost pure light, angel-like. They reached graduation status and their game of duality was done. Earth was next, and the Pleiadians' job was to adjust the DNA of the human to where it could hold the divinity of who we are. They did that by landing here and staying here, literally marrying their biology with ours. That's how our game of free choice, choice between dark and light, alignment or nonalignment with our soul began. The Pleiadians stayed as teachers for the first civilizations and are still here in their light bodies, within the nodes and nulls of the planet. There are 12 node and null pairs on the grids of Gaia, that were set up as Pleiadian time capsules. If humanity ever chose to wake up, these nodes and nulls would be activated and calibrated and out would pour the wisdom of our collective Star Akash. Meaning all the inventions, solutions and technologies we ever invented in other places, other games of duality, would gradually become available in the field of potentials, on the grids of this planet. And then anyone could tune into these potentials and channel them into 3D reality. Scientists, musicians, healers, politicians, artists, ... all would start bringing forth new compassionate, enlightened ways for awakening humanity.[4]

My cells dance with these words. My whole being recognizes the truth presented. I embrace the potential for peace on Earth. I embrace the potential of an enlightened Earth. I can't wait for the future to manifest. I am also joyfully expecting new discoveries within my own being and merging with the petals of my soul. It fills me with gratitude and joy to be able to be part of this grand awakening.

Time Capsules in Cetaceans

Nodes and nulls are not the only places where Pleiadian time capsules reside. They exist within each of us and also, you guessed it, the cetaceans.

Here are Kryon's words, "When the Pleiadians came, in all love and all appropriateness, as a graduate ascended race, to plant the seeds on this planet of free choice, they didn't just plant them in human beings. Use your imagination. That's why you're in love with them. It's why in certain cases and in excursions you've taken, in special places around the Earth, you can get into the water and the dolphins will come to you. Did you ever think of that? What is it that they are attracted to? I'll let you think about that one. There is more coming dear ones and as this planet evolves, we will be able to tell you a little more about the role that they play. But you already know of their sacredness. You already know about the whales and the dolphins. The cetaceans are like a living library. They are important to you. They hold an energy that is part of you. They are one of the 9."[5]

I want to share what my intuition is telling me about cetacean time capsules. All time capsules work as an inter-related network and it's only to our physical eyes that they seem separate. Awakening and activation within one time capsule reverberates throughout the system. In other words, when humans open up and start activating the layers of their quantum DNA, there is stirring within the cetaceans as well as the nodes and nulls in the mountains. It happens on both the individual and collective level, and that's why it's so complex. It always occurs at the perfect time. For example, let's take a scientist, who wakes up to an ancient wisdom inside. His time capsule activates, and he receives an inspiration, an invention that will be able to help millions of people. But it can't go mainstream until the consciousness of humanity reaches a certain level, which is when the nodes and nulls will respond in a way that will allow his invention to be received by humanity.

So, what purpose do dolphins and whales have in the time capsule system? Kryon says they are the back-up system for the Crystalline grid of the planet, meaning they help to store everything that has ever happened here on earth.[6] But what if they are also a window into what's happened on other planets, a window into our

Star Akash? I believe time capsules serve as communication devices, where the wisdom of who you've been elsewhere in the galaxy, can be transmitted here to support you in this incarnation. You can see dolphins and whales as "star librarians," that look at your energy and what you're ready for and go find an appropriate "book" in your Star Akash – an experience you had on another planet that can empower you in this lifetime.

I passionately believe we are to gradually claim this role for ourselves and become our own memory keepers. I believe dolphin time capsules carry energetic codes, instruction manuals, on how to navigate this multidimensional reality. In the next chapter, I talk about 7 dolphin points on the human body that can help us embody our dolphin qualities and explore our quantum nature.

Songs of the whales can be heard underwater from hundreds of miles away. They talk to each other over great distances. I believe that their songs also have a multidimensional part that travels all around the Earth, it goes in the ocean or on land. It wraps the planet in a gentle blanket of tales from the stars. Do you hear their quantum songs? Do you recognize the stories that they sing in light, revealing bit by bit of who you've been, your beauty, your lineage? Are you ready to receive this gift?

Groote Eylandt Story – Multidimensional Split?

I described the human soul as a flower with different petals, each petal carrying its own flavor of love. When your higher self (the center of the flower) says, "I AM," it resonates throughout every petal: your human consciousness, your guides, your inner dolphin, the mountains, your enlightened incarnations from past and future, and much more. While this is complex by itself, now imagine every flower petal being able to go and experience its own journey – explore different dimensions, incarnations, and realities. Petals will always be part of the flower of the soul, they all tie back to its original I AM, but you may find them experiencing another reality in a seemingly separate way. Since we as humans tend to forget who we really are, we might encounter a petal of our soul, and think it is not in any way connected to us. Are you still following me?

Do you understand that means you might come in contact with a part of your soul that could be embodied in a dolphin you've just swam with? Could it be then that you indeed are one AND the other, you are the I AM in both of you. If that is true, it would certainly explain the creation story of the Groote Eylandt people of Northern Australia from chapter 4, wouldn't it? The story talks about a smaller kind of dolphins, who were all, but one, killed by tiger sharks. Dolphins' souls rose out of the ocean and became humans. Ganadja, the only remaining dolphin, gave birth to a new, bigger kind of dolphins and then joined humans. You could say the story describes the soul split – the multidimensional petals embarking on their own journeys, some of them experiencing human and other dolphin realities. The story does make sure though, that we understand how related we really are – same soul, different journeys.

Just to really stretch your imagination, here's another idea. Your soul is represented as a metaphor of a flower. What about everybody else? You're not here alone, remember? If there's billions of souls, what do they create? Why, a beautiful FIELD of flowers, wouldn't you agree? So, I'll let you think about this one, "What kind of resonance is then created, when The Field says, 'I AM?'" Do you understand that in that moment, every flower acknowledges it is part of The Field? The flowers know that The Field sustains them. They celebrate the dirt and the minerals, they celebrate morning dew and the sunshine that allows them to grow. The Field never says to a flower, "You have to grow in certain way." The Field simply loves each and every flower and celebrates the beauty of every single petal, because The Field knows, it is all a part of it.

Here's my definition of God: the resonance of "I AM" through The Field of the soul-flowers. God is love that sustains and allows for growth of souls in infinite compassion, celebration, and expansion. Hawaiians have a word, "Aloha," which means both "Hello" and "Goodbye," but also "Love." "Ha" is the breath of life, that is flowing through every living thing, including plants, rocks and mountains. "Alo" means presence, so when you put them together, you acknowledge the presence of "Ha" or the breath of the Creator in everything. And you find "Aloha." You find love!

Are Dolphins Really from Sirius?

There's a consensus in New Age circles that dolphins come from Sirius, meaning, their souls come from one of Earth's nearest stars. Sirius can be seen as a bright blue white star in the night sky near the Orion constellation.

I have to admit, I didn't know anything about it until many years into my journey with dolphins. Why would dolphins' origins be important? Here's my understanding based on Kryon's work. Sirius is one of places where the game of duality took place before the Pleiadeas, which means they reached their collective enlightenment a very long time ago and then helped Pleiadians on their journey. In other words, they are the ancestors of the ancestors, or as Kryon calls them, the grandparents. While parents (Pleiadians) are more concerned about kid's behavior, learning and progress, grandparents just want to have fun! Now that sounds a lot like dolphins to me!

I would explain it this way, the part of you that has reached enlightenment in the star system Sirius, in that moment merged with your Higher Self, and became free of time and space. Which means, it can be present with you in any moment as your guide; a loving, compassionate force next to you. This part of you is inextricably linked with the cetaceans, who are not just from Sirius (same as you are not just from any one planet), but for the purpose of our evolution and especially for the post-2012 awakening time, they carry Sirius frequency within them.

I've found over the years that dolphins use play as a way to distract our minds, while other things happen multidimensionally. It happens so innocently. You're swimming with them, giggling as you're playing together, and then, "Bam!" you get hit by the most profound feeling of love, communication that goes deeper than words can even describe. Every cell of your body downloads new insights and comes into amazing alignment, you literally are changed forever. Doesn't that sound like wise grandparents saying, "We will transfer our wisdom through play."

Exploring the Sirius subject, I found it's not all "New Agey" after all. It comes from ancient traditions of certain African tribes, most well-known being the Dogon tribe from Mali in Western Africa. They became so famous that Leonard Nemoy included them in a show called "In Search Of" back in the 70s.[7] Why? According to French anthropologists that worked with them in the 1930s, their tribal stories tell of a landing of spaceships from an invisible star, that circles around a bright blue star in our night sky, Sirius. It turns out years later, that their knowledge was confirmed by science. Sirius is a binary star system, with a white dwarf star called Sirius B, invisible to the naked eye.

Dogons shared that the beings that landed were called "Nommo," and had kind of an aquatic look to them, like dolphins or fish, but were standing upright. Nommo revealed the secrets of the Universe and stayed with Dogons as teachers (sounds familiar?). Among other things, Dogon drawings show things from our solar system, that couldn't be observed without a telescope, like rings of Saturn and Jupiter's moons.

I knew I had to include "Sirius stuff" in this chapter, after I'd read a quote channeled by Alcazar, a Stargate guide. Stargate is a physical structure that represents a higher dimensional consciousness we are all invited to work with. It was channeled through Prageet Harris under the instructions of Alcazar, who guides people into very profound meditations to connect with a personal etheric Stargate and 12-dimensional energy field, where you then meet with ascended masters and different star races.[8]

A dear friend of mine, who just finished a Stargate intensive in Mount Shasta, came to visit me and told me that, "Alcazar said dolphins and whales are not going to be here forever." And I thought, "That actually makes perfect sense! If we are to take their gift, which is a part of our soul and embody everything they carry, then their job would be finished, and they would be free to go."

I wrote to Julieanne, who co-channels Alcazar with Prageet and she was happy to share the exact channeling with me to be able to transcribe the words. Here's what he said:

"As you know, the whales and the dolphins come from that place. The consciousness of those beings comes from this place, Sirius. In the future, when they have completed their project of holding this information for humanity, when you awaken more and more and start receiving back this information from them, the whales and then the dolphins will actually leave your Earth. Do not be sad, when that happens. It will be time to celebrate that humanity has arisen out of unconsciousness and is accelerating into full awareness on your Earth."[9]

Don't you just love it when information coming from different sources aligns? I love opening up through my own intuition first, writing about it and then finding confirmation from the outside.

Dolphins and whales will not actually leave this planet. It might seem so in the physical world, but, that's when your connection with them will be stronger than ever, you will carry them around swimming in your energy field and time capsules will be fully activated and calibrated. And that's when this book will complete its mission – humans will merge with their inner dolphin.

To conclude this chapter, I want to share words from Credo Mutwa, a Zulu elder from South Africa, who speaks about cetaceans with high reverence. "The Zulu people say, 'The knowledge comes from the sea.' Our people believe that many many many centuries ago, a race of intelligent creatures of various kinds placed the human race onto this world in which we are in exile. The members of this race went into the sea to become what we today call dolphins. Over the centuries, dolphins and whales sent knowledge via dreams to human beings. The whales told us all about God. The dolphins told us all about wisdom and art and other forms of positive creativity. We, the black people, believe that these dolphins are not fish, they are 'Amahengeto,' the saviors. They are people. They have a kingdom under the sea. They have stories that they tell their children. And they have hopes for the future. We say that they came with their great emperor, "Wowane," from the star called Sirius by the white people, many many many millenniums ago."[10]

I am blown away by how this puzzle comes together – the ancients, channeled sources, my own intuition and everything I've experienced, it all aligns in a beautiful, synchronistic way. Thank you for reading and being on this journey with me. My heart is overflowing with gratitude as I write these words. I feel honored to be able to uncover what has always been there. Do you see why masters say to us, "Look inside?" Truly, that's where the magnificence of our being is revealed. I breathe it all in and say the words that Alcazar, the Stargate guide, instructed us to say often, "Thank you, bring me more!"

And so it is.

• CHAPTER 7 •

Inner Dolphin Awakening

I WAS STANDING IN A MURKY kitchen in a little coastal town in Croatia. My transformation was complete. I had become a dolphin.

"Now what?" I asked myself as I observed how I could freely transition from my human being to my dolphin being. I went on a walk around town, breathing in the evening air. I walked past a night club and right in front of my eyes a brawl erupted, with people screaming and hitting each other. I got really scared and started to quickly walk away, trying to save my skin. But then, with a deep conscious breath, the dolphin came in and... it didn't care! It had too much fun paying attention to the way the light was reflecting on the water.

"What about the fight?" I asked.

"Just swim away." said my inner dolphin.

A couple of dolphin breaths later the fear was gone. It was too exciting to explore and enjoy the little sights of beauty. Why would anyone try and focus on a fight? For some reason, that's exactly what humans do. But as soon as I allowed myself to remember my inner dolphin, the whole situation shifted.

That's how I learned the first big lesson of my experience, *you always have a choice!* What are you going to focus on? Now this might be the biggest gift of our multidimensional nature – within the numerous levels of our being there's always a part of us that is not focused in drama, fear and separation. Do you see the beauty of this? The big revelation here is, don't try and fix the human. *Just build a bridge to another piece of your soul!*

You're not trying to stop the human part from feeling what it's feeling. You're not trying to change it, or even worse, conquer yourself. You take a deep breath and remember what else is there. Remember the flower of your soul. Remember the multiple levels of your being, all carrying your name in light. Remember the gifts you left for yourself on the Crystalline grid and in time capsules. You truly have a support system like no other and all it takes is embracing it.

And that's what this chapter is all about. While the main focus is the Inner Dolphin Awakening, which is a system to build a bridge to the cetacean part of your soul, you are invited to become a quantum explorer yourself. My wish is that this chapter be an inspiration on your journey to discover your sacred nature and remember the beautiful flower of your soul.

The Puzzle

Soon after I got back home from Azores, I had a dream where I met with Marinella again, the beautiful goddess-like woman who facilitated my dolphin awakening. In my dreams, she gently touched the corners of my eyes and said, "Dolphin eyes. Remember the dolphin eyes? You see the beauty and blessings of life." This dream was the first piece of a puzzle that would start to be revealed in the months to come.

The next piece was a session with a psychic reader, whom I wanted to ask a few questions about the direction of my life. When wondering whether to take a class on healing technique I was interested in, the psychic's guidance was very clear, "You are not to study other techniques anymore. You need to develop your own."

This answer left me confused. Me, developing something? But how? I had no idea.

So, I decided to put a friend on a massage table and experiment. I was just playing with the energy, moving my hands over her field and observing what happened. And then an idea popped into my mind, "I wonder if I can find her inner dolphin?" I focused my hands over her nose and imagined it changing and then her mouth and eyes. That's when my dreams and Marinella's words came back to me, "Dolphin eyes. You see the beauty and blessings of life." I realized dolphins' eyes are wired for beauty.

"Hm, could it be that then each body part represents something?" I wondered.

I returned to the nose and as I tuned in, I could see a dolphin underwater, exploring his environment and I suddenly understood the energy, "Curiosity, dolphin nose represents curiosity!" I almost screamed with excitement. I followed the transformation from one point to the next, downloading meanings and energies, seeing pictures and colors. It was such a natural, easy process.

1. Dolphin Nose – Curiosity
2. Dolphin Smile – Joy
3. Dolphin Eyes – Beauty
4. Blowhole – Soul Breath
5. Pectoral Fins – Telepathy

6. Dorsal Fin – Multidimensionality
7. Dolphin Tail – Gaia

By the end of it I had seven dolphin points, a route for the interdimensional journey from human to inner dolphin. All of a sudden, the most quantum event of my life had a form others could connect to, I was excited to see what followed.

And then... nothing happened. I had all this beautiful information and I didn't know what to do with it. I knew I was not to offer healing sessions. This was not about healing, it was about empowerment. I trusted that the next step would be revealed in at the right time, what I didn't know was it would take 4 years.

I needed to collect other pieces of the puzzle, travel to Maui for the choir and then journey across the South Pacific with the tones to truly integrate my Lemurian self. Finally, after going to Shasta and beginning my new life, I was ready to move the energy. I started writing the process down, trying to find a clear way to present the material, but something was still missing.

Talking to Your Cells

I found out Kryon was coming to Portland, forty-five minutes away from where I lived.

Two big pieces of information came from Kryon in that seminar. First was Lee's slide about 9 Levels of Human Soul that I spoke about in the previous chapter.

And the second part was Kryon's message for this new time (post Winter Solstice 2012), explaining the importance of talking to the Innate (body intelligence), "Learn how to build affirmations that are positive. Get in touch with the body through whatever process that comes your way. You are ready to communicate to the smart body. Now, the beauty of this is the following: You don't have to convince Innate of anything. It knows! It has been waiting for the call! As soon as it sees the progress that you have made in your consciousness, it's a done deal. Did you hear that? Innate knows who you are! After all, it's the smart body. But it doesn't know until you make the call."[1]

I experienced an "Aha" moment while listening to these words. If I can talk to my Innate in a form of affirmations, what about inner dolphin affirmations? Could this be the missing piece, one that allows for a bridge to be built to that part of my soul? If yes, then anyone could do it!

My understanding, which is reflected in the words of Kryon, is that affirmations will never work unless they are true, meaning you have to understand that the energy you're trying to evoke is already there, the potential for a different reality is waiting for your embodiment. So, you're not trying to convince yourself or your Innate of something, you're simply activating a reality that was already there, in your multidimensional field.

So here I was, with a beautiful map of seven dolphin points on the human body, having just received the message, "Use the affirmations!" It was so simple. I sat down and tuned into each dolphin point and as I felt the energy, the words just started flowing. Out came the guided journey that you're about to experience yourself. Before we start, there's one important thing we need to do. I believe nothing will really shift, and I'm talking about deep, profound changes in consciousness and understanding, until we bring in the foundation for interdimensional discovery, self-love.

Self-love: Telepathy Within Your Own Being

Have you heard this message before? Love yourself! It seems like everybody is talking about it. Why is it so important to love ourselves?

Here's my view: Do you remember how in the third chapter, I described what makes telepathy possible? I called it a bridge between the hearts. Love builds a bridge that then allows for a signal to travel from one being to the other. So now look at what happens with self-love, it builds a bridge between different parts of your multidimensional self. In other words: If you don't love yourself, you will never be able to open the door to your soul fully. Self-love allows for telepathy within your own being!

And here's the best part: Self-love is already a hundred percent present. Your soul already has an immense love and appreciation for you. Gaia already loves you more than you could ever imagine. Dolphins and whales could jump for the pure joy of seeing you. So, dear human, your part is not to try to love yourself, but to remember, allow and receive the love that is already there.

It truly is the biggest shift we can make. In the moment of experiencing self-love, you open the door to everything you are, the flower of your soul. Suddenly, messages appear, intuition gets stronger and abundance flows, naturally. It's not about asking, it's simply about receiving.

Exercise 5: Hug Yourself

Think about a very dear friend of yours, or somebody you love dearly. Imagine not seeing them in a while and then sharing a hug with them. A hug like that would likely last for at least 20 seconds, and would be filled with the joy of reunion. You wouldn't want it to end. This is the kind of a feeling you want to recreate, this time hugging yourself.

Gently place your right hand on your left shoulder and your left hand on your right shoulder and close your eyes. Bring in the feeling of reunion described above, and hold yourself with the same intensity. This hug is a physical manifestation of self-love.

Now remember the flower of your soul. Remember the numerous petals on that flower, representing your guides, inner dolphin, and enlightened star incarnations. They are all there to love you, dear human, exactly the way you are in this moment. You are important, celebrated and known. You are part of the family.

All you need to do is start receiving. You can do that by simply saying, "Yes!" every time you breathe in. "Yes, I receive your love. I remember the love I have for myself."

Stay in this space. Allow for love to flow. Allow for appreciation to flow. Self-love is already a hundred percent present. Just receive it with every breath.

Doing this every day, you will notice that self-love will become part of your day. It will come out in unexpected moments, while driving your car, eating a meal, talking to a friend. It is always there, and you can allow yourself to feel it whenever you want.

7 Dolphin Points on Your Body

I hope you are as excited as I am to come to this part of the book. My intent is for this information to be shared and to become a useful tool in humanity's multi-dimensional tool box. I believe there is much more to come and we're only tapping into the first resources available. I hope this information is a catalyst for new insights and revelations.

Inner Dolphin Awakening is designed to gently guide you from one dolphin point to the next, allowing you to feel the essence of each point and inviting you to start bringing it here, to this reality. As affirmations are said out loud, your Innate hears them and cooperates in shifting the energy.

In its most simple form, this journey only takes a few minutes, as you touch each of the points and say the affirmations, so it's perfect to do it first thing in the morning. I thought this is what I will give you here... until the dolphin presence, I've channeled in previous chapter came back. It turns out they wanted to personally guide you on the journey of Inner Dolphin Awakening.

"Dear human, we are ready to guide you through this process. First and foremost, you are loved and appreciated for coming here and opening up to this experience. It is a part of you. Like we said before, your sacredness wouldn't be the same without it. Remember, the intention is to have fun and enjoy.

You are about to open your consciousness. You are about to allow a memory of how it feels to be in more than one place at the same time. But really, it is all inside you. You are not trying to reach out to something that you wished existed. It is as simple as taking a breath, and allowing yourself to be guided in this expansion. Ready?

Deep breath. Relax your whole being. Smile.

1. DOLPHIN NOSE – Curiosity

Gently touch your nose. Remember the dolphin nose. Say out loud, for every cell to hear,

"I am curious, and I love to explore. I awaken the dolphin within."

2. DOLPHIN SMILE – Joy

Gently touch the corners of your mouth. Remember the dolphin smile. Say and really feel the essence of these words,

"I am joyful, and I love life. I awaken the dolphin within."

How do you like it so far? Do you feel what's coming through? Trust it. It is yours. Let's continue. Deep breath again.

3. DOLPHIN EYES – Beauty

Touch the corners of your eyes. Have you heard that your eyes are a mirror of your soul? What would you see, if your soul was looking out? Feel that as you remember the dolphin eyes,

"I see the beauty and blessings of life. I awaken the dolphin within."

Ah, thank you so much, dear human. Thank you for allowing yourself to experience the beauty of this process.

4. DOLPHIN BLOWHOLE – Breath

Place your attention on top of your head. Gently touch your crown. Remember the dolphin blowhole and see yourself taking a breath through your crown and say,

"I breathe deeply. I use my breath to bring in my soul. I awaken the dolphin within."

Continue breathing deeply. Continue coming up for air, diving back down into the waters of life. You are in the right place.

5. PECTORAL FINS – Telepathy

Pectoral fins. Your hands open outwards and your elbows press into the sides of your body. You keep breathing deeply, but now you become aware of your heart. Do you notice how your hand posture opens your heart, automatically? Yes.

"My heart is always open. I explore telepathy and interspecies communication. I awaken the dolphin within."

You are not alone. You are surrounded by beautiful beings of light ... and you have a dolphin family. When you remember your inner dolphin, your heart becomes part of the pod. Can you feel that right now? We are out there, swimming in the ocean and, yet, we are present in your heart, at the same time. Telepathy is easy. Just allow yourself to feel this connection. We are always with you. We have gifts for you and your heart can start receiving now. Are you ready?

6. DORSAL FIN – Multidimensionality

There's always more. Your beautiful being is grander than you think. There are levels of your beautiful consciousness, that go beyond what your human brain can conceive. It's okay to open up, step by step. But know one thing, you are far grander than you think. This is what dorsal fin reminds you of. You came from the stars. Gently touch your tailbone and say,

"I am a multidimensional being, filled with light, color, and sound. Self-love builds a bridge to my quantum nature. I remember my star origins."

Beautiful human, if you only knew your lineage, if you only remembered where you've been. It fills us with joy and gratitude, to share this journey with you. Are you ready for more?

7. DOLPHIN TAIL – Gaia

It is time to bring this beauty and this magnificence, that has your name on it to this beautiful planet, Gaia. She is here in service. She is here to support you and nourish you and take care of you. She is your beautiful mother, your humanity's mother. Everything you see around you, was created for you, for your experience. Can you feel gratitude now for this beautiful planet? The story doesn't end there. Feel your feet and remember the dolphin tail. Realize that Gaia, this beautiful, infinite, loving consciousness lives within you as well. You are part of Gaia. She is part of you. You are connected through eternity.

"I embody Gaia. I am one with the soul of the planet. I awaken the dolphin within."

Can you feel the transformation dear human? You are doing precious work. All of a sudden you are in two places at the same time. Your consciousness is fine with it. You embody the beauty of your human self and also your dolphin self. They are both here for you, to navigate through this life with ease and grace. Remember the dolphin codes. Remember the dolphin love. Remember the dolphin joy. And most importantly, remember the beauty of your soul.

"I am that I am. I awaken the dolphin within."

And the bridge is built. Use it often dear human. Use it in any way that serves you. You are precious. Let's play today, ok?

Aloha e, dolphins"

Take a moment to notice how you feel after activating and feeling the dolphin points? Do you notice any changes within you, any difference in your energy? I would say practice makes perfect, but that's not really accurate in this case. Because you are simply opening to a part of your multidimensional self, and practice only makes what was always there easier to perceive and allow. So, it would be better to say that practice makes the walls between the dimensions thinner.

One way to play with these points is to find two dolphin points that have the strongest resonance for you in that moment. How I do this is I scan my body and feel into each dolphin point, usually there is one that is radiating the strongest. This is the point I focus on and take a few deep breaths to receive its energy. (It is interesting to observe how simply focusing on one dolphin quality can completely shift my energy). And then I look for another point that resonates with the first one, a "support point" that makes it shine even brighter. I find the second point by focusing on the first one and simultaneously scanning all the other ones at the same time. What happens is one will simply "step out" or "volunteer," for a lack of better word. Together they create what I call a "power two", two dolphin points communicating with and empowering each other. The most amazing thing is to then observe this relationship: in what way can they work together and bring each other into a higher resonance. When I do that, I find they click into place and create an energy that stays with me for hours. Try it!

Here is my invitation: To dedicate a part of your day to this practice of opening and remembering. Perhaps take a few minutes in the morning when you first wake up, allowing yourself to really feel the points as you say the affirmations. My wish is that every moment you spend with the points deepens your sense of joy throughout your day.

Inner Child Meets Inner Dolphin

This is a powerful extension of Inner Dolphin Awakening – do it with your inner child! See your inner child in your heart as you travel through the dolphin points, have not only your Innate, but also the child in you, listen to and feel the affirmations.

Inner child is that beautiful part of you that stays with you throughout your life, there to remind you of playfulness, presence, vulnerability, and joy of being in the moment. When inner child is hurt, lonely or angry, she/he can't do its part to allow you to embrace life fully, so the idea is to meet your child where she/he is and slowly create a safe space and a loving relationship. When their feelings are recognized, expressed, and healed you will realize inner child becomes a source of constant love for life, inspiration, and wonder.

Doesn't it make sense that inner child and inner dolphin would create a special resonance together? It took me a while to put two and two together. I have worked a lot with my inner child over the years and was wondering why would we need two parts that are both joyful and love life. I hadn't realized I was seeing them as separate, until one day my inner child was dancing in my heart as I was saying affirmations out loud – he loved it! That was an "Aha" moment for me, realizing my inner child is the part of me most ready and willing to attune to the dolphin frequencies. Isn't that logical? Inner child can help you remember your multidimensional nature!

As I was feeling into my soul flower, the representation of many parts of my sacredness, I saw my inner dolphin as one of the petals, but my inner child went straight into the middle, to the I AM. This brought about another realization – inner child that lives in your heart creates a direct portal to your I AM!

• CHAPTER 8 •

Opening Cetacean Time Capsules

THIS IS THE THIRD TIME I'll be talking about time capsules. In numerology for number 3 (a catalytic number) means it's time for action. The further I came with writing this book, the more time capsules wouldn't leave me alone. It felt like their energy demanded my attention.

That's the reason I decided to spend extra time on this subject and soon a new clarity started to emerge. Could it be that cetacean time capsules and Inner Dolphin Awakening are connected?

I returned to reading what Kryon said about time capsules and there was one part where my intuition lit up. In 2014, in Mt.Shasta, Kryon shared that time capsules within the nodes and nulls are like antennas – receivers of energy and information, "12 pairs of push-pull energy, called time capsules. The time capsules contain nothing. The nomenclature of time capsule is given for you, a metaphor. Something is there, and it has to do with time and I'll tell you why. Because the time is NOW! Those capsules, when they are opened, are like doors and don't transmit anything. They are receivers... the way push-pull energy works, [it's] transmitted from the Great Central Source to the planets of free choice which have gone into ascension status, which all have receivers. You are like a pressure cooker without a receiver. You had to pass that marker, dear civilization, dear human being, before your receivers could pop up and start the process in year one."[1]

Furthermore, in Kryon book 14 there's an explanation on how the change in the grids of the planets through nodes and nulls, is then picked up by the time capsules in our DNA. Kryon states it happens through the non-linear part of the DNA, the 90% of the code that used to be called "junk." "Science now understands that this 90 percent is information – a manual – a control panel for the genes ... This 90 percent is like trillions of antennas in your body, ready to receive information and then rewrite the manual via the changes in your grids."[2]

As I listened to these words a light bulb turned on in my mind. Could it be that dolphin points on our body are like antennas as well? Could it be that fine tuning them would allow for us to start receiving personal multidimensional information from cetaceans, start experiencing what time capsules have to offer?

In the sixth chapter, I called dolphins and whales "star librarians," bringing to us the gifts of our Star Akash. I also said we are to gradually claim this role for ourselves. In other words, what if we have to BECOME joyful, multidimensional beings to be able to RECEIVE multidimensional information?

This means that the more you embody the dolphin qualities, the clearer the signal from the stars becomes. You will start to know and remember things from your Star Akash and claim them as you walk on this planet. This chapter, therefore, is all about fine tuning the dolphin points. In each section, I present three different perspectives: mine, numerological[3] and dolphins' (channeled). They all combine to give you a bigger picture and invite you to dive deeper! Are you ready?

Let's first set the energy for this exploration. Please join me in affirming out loud, "I am ready to start receiving the gifts of the time capsules. I receive what dolphins and whales carry and I utilize dolphin points as multidimensional receivers. I will calibrate and fine tune this gift to allow for a complete remembrance of my Star Akash. I am ready."

1. Curiosity

"I am curious, and I love to explore."

Curiosity has always been one of the most known dolphin characteristics. When you get in the water with them, they will come to see you and check you out. While this is obvious, there is a theme that has been repeated throughout this book. Dolphins' curiosity goes much deeper than what they see, because they have an ability to perceive multidimensional parts of your soul. So, when you are invited to explore what dolphin nose represents, understand you are invited to use curiosity to "look behind" and start perceiving the bigger picture. That's when curiosity becomes one of the most important tools you have.

Can you use this tool when you talk to another person and all you see is their human personality? Activate your dolphin nose and start exploring the multidimensional reality. This person, right in front of you has an amazing, rich Akash, infinite soul and numerous spiritual gifts that are waiting to be revealed in a perfect time. The colors of his/her Merkabah are spectacular and are talking to you on so many levels. Are you curious enough to open to the world behind? How about nature, rocks, trees, and other animals? When you activate this dolphin point, there will be discovery after discovery. Enjoy the ride!

Numerology of 1

Number 1 represents new beginnings. Every time you connect with this dolphin point you start opening doors to new things. It is also the first of the 7 dolphin points on the human body, representing the beginning of the Inner Dolphin Awakening journey. Nothing will happen unless you first become curious, saying, "Inner dolphin? Tell me more!"

Dolphins on Curiosity

Focus your attention on your nose. Can you allow yourself to be guided by what your nose represents, curiosity? It is such a precious energy, it's very simple, so simple it might trick some people into believing it's not important. Let us say this, it is very important. It is the first dolphin point, the first energy dolphins wish to share with humanity and like every other one, it is actually interdimensional energy, meaning once tapped into, it will start affecting you way beyond your physical presence.

Curiosity can take you out of any situation and open up a field of new possibilities you didn't know existed. Curiosity alone can let you expand and leave the old you behind. Curiosity is the secret to new beginnings.

So, here's a little challenge. Can you go into a space that is well known to you? Like your room or office or supermarket you go to daily. And just close your eyes, take a deep breath, feel the dolphin nose and say, "I am curious, and I love to explore." Then open your eyes, keep the energy going and see what comes up for you. In this space, that you know intimately, can you allow yourself to see in a new way? Can you be curious enough to do that? Where does your nose guide you?

You see, your world is really not the same as it was yesterday. Your being is not the same as it was yesterday. Everything is constantly moving and reshaping itself. Your belief keeps it looking the same. But it's not. If you practice this, you will start realizing that curiosity has the power to take you out of your limiting belief. It has the power to allow you to start witnessing the flow of life as simply that: the flow. It is like water, flowing itself, molding itself, ever-changing. Be curious. It is the first step into freedom. It is the first step to see beyond your limitations. It is the first step to see beyond this 3-dimensional reality.

2. Joy

"I am joyful, and I love life."

There's a moment when you wake up from your sleep in the morning, a moment before you really remember your humanness – your mind hasn't started working yet. That peaceful moment is a huge opportunity. If you say an affirmation in that moment, it can shift your energy profoundly. My choice every morning is to dedicate that moment to joy. I wake up and before I even open my eyes I say to my cells, "I am joyful!" and then I observe what happens in my body. Dolphins have me going even further with an exercise they called "A Wave of Joy," and they will explain that in a moment.

I believe our level of joy is very much connected to the amount of passion we have in our lives, that's why the second part of affirmation is "... and I love life." When you discover things that make your heart sing, make you forget about everything else, and immerse yourself in the present moment, you realize that joy was always there, underneath your normal human experience. Through passion you connect with what you are meant to be doing here, in this lifetime, in this body. Living with passion, following your joy, aligns you with your soul in the best possible way. Joy then becomes a catalyst for deep spiritual awakening and fulfillment.

Numerology of 2

Number 2 represents duality, our choice between light and dark, remembering and forgetting. So why would joy be connected to this number? Because it helps you transcend duality. Joy is a reminder of your multidimensional state. Joy is the vibration of your soul that willingly entered this body, this game of duality, to experience everything our planet has to offer.

Dolphins on Joy

Ah, joy. If there is one simple favorite subject of ours, it is joy. The funniest thing is that there isn't much to say about it. So, let's do this, take a deep breath and smile. Now allow that feeling of joy, that your smile represents, to slowly start spreading throughout your body. Cell by cell, a smile spreads around. It starts around your mouth and slowly, it's like a game of telephone, cells tell each other about it. Hear them whisper at first, saying to each other, "We're joyful, we're joyful!" and the more it spreads the louder it gets, "We're joyful, we're joyful." Before you know it, every cell will be celebrating in what is its natural state. So, here is a premise: Cells want to be happy. Cells want to celebrate life. Cells want to dance and feel excitement and gratitude. But their first job is to be of service. Who do they serve? Your consciousness. So, what happens, when you worry and fear?

They love you so much they are willing to do anything you ask them. They will recreate your body to whatever form you wish. Are you listening? How much time do you take daily to laugh and have fun? Just look at us. Have you heard stories of dolphins and what happened when people spend time with them? Did anyone mention laughing and playing and jumping for joy? Do you think that just happens, because we are different, or are we actually choosing to experience joy, spreading it from our smile throughout our bodies, like waves of happiness, like waves of joy? You know the answer to that.

So, here's an invitation: Can you wake up every day, and first thing, smile and observe the wave of happiness spread from cell to cell. Only after you're done with that do you start thinking about your day and what adventures await. And remember, no matter what is happening and no matter what your mind tells you, you always have the ability to move those corners of your mouth, just a little and the smile will start showing itself. Not to mention, you will start finding you are becoming more beautiful because of it too! Thank you!

3. Beauty

"I see the beauty and blessings of life."

I often have spontaneous experiences of intense beauty. They come suddenly without prior notice. Sometimes they are connected to what I'm thinking and other times they are connected to the beauty of Gaia. They are directly related to the amount of joy and gratitude I am allowing myself to feel. When a moment of beauty arrives, it fills me up with an amazing energy of bliss and I start seeing everything outside of me as a more vibrant, coherent presence. I can see the higher order of things, how everything pulsates in the beautiful, cosmic scheme of life. I believe dolphins are in this state most of the time, and the intention here is for us to do the same.

There is a simple way to start seeing the beauty and blessings of life and it's what every master did: become a blessing yourself! Simply raise your hand and start blessing things around you. You can start with yourself, your body, your organs, your cells. Continue with everything in your surroundings. Then close your eyes and start blessing your relationships and whatever else comes up for you, even your challenges and hardships. Bless everything. That is the only way to find a gift in everything, even the hard stuff. You will notice how your energy changes and how, when you open your eyes, you can start observing a different, more beautiful reality around you, that now carries the sweetness of your blessing.

Numerology of 3

Number 3 is a catalyst, meaning it represents an energy that can change everything around it, while it stays the same. Beauty can be a catalyst for the remembrance of your soul. When you focus on beauty, you start to increase your vibration and perceive the sacredness inside.

Dolphins on Beauty

This brings us to next dolphin point, your eyes. Can you touch the corner of your eyes lightly and allow yourself to feel these words, "I am beautiful. I see my beauty and I see it reflected in everything around me. All is one. All is within me and I am everywhere. I awaken the dolphin within." You see, this affirmation caught Jan by surprise. He expected the affirmation he always uses, but if you go back and read it, and then read what we said here, you will see we're talking about the same thing. Because you can't see beauty outside if you don't see it in yourself first.

It is a gift to be able to go beyond what you think was there, meaning beyond seeing yourself as just a mere human, having a single body that allows you to experience this and that while it slowly gets old. Think again. We really want you to start understanding yourself as a multi-perceptional being within the multidimensional existence. Because you see, as you do this, you will move a step closer to your higher self, for your higher self is the totality of everything you've ever been.

Seeing the beauty is more about understanding who you really are, than it is about trying to search for little perfect shapes within the physical. Perfection is already there. You are already seeing it, but you have to allow yourself to change the definition of you. It is a beautiful game, but only a part of you is within it.

So, let's do this, take a deep breath and release everything, past-present-future, your understanding of what is and what isn't. And then, take another breath straight into the white light of your consciousness, and allow it to permeate. Then ask this consciousness to look through your eyes. What does it see, what do you see as an expanded, beautiful, sacred presence? Indeed. Practice this often and you will remember what's on the other side. Blessings!

4. Breath

"I use my breath to bring in my soul. I use my breath to bring in the celebration of Spirit."

Conscious breath has been my most faithful companion on the journey of self-discovery. It comes as no surprise to me that it's such an important part of the dolphin teaching. Dolphins have to take each breath consciously, they choose a moment when they come to the surface and breathe.

Can you close your eyes and imagine that for a moment, being underwater for a while and then swimming up, and feeling how the freshness of the air and life force enter through your crown?

On my path, I was strongly influenced by an amazing woman, Norma Delaney, and her practice of deep, compassionate breath, that goes all the way down into your belly and fills it up like a balloon. This breath starts to integrate aspects of you that are hurt and forgotten, as you invite in compassion from your soul.[4]

In a similar way, a dolphin breath that comes in through your crown chakra, reminds you to start consciously connecting to higher levels of your being – and bring them here.

Numerology of 4

Number 4 is a Gaia number, practical and structural. When you combine this with a breath that opens into spiritual levels, the result is profound. You are invited to bring your soul onto this planet, into this body in a practical, grounded way – with every breath.

Dolphins on Breathing

You will start to notice that the dolphin points interact with each other, merge one into the other and create a certain kind of resonance when looked at together. So, this dolphin point, your blowhole is really a part of every other one. For you see, without the breath of God nothing would really exist on this planet or any other planet for that matter. Feel that as you take the next breath. Acknowledge the sacredness of breathing.

This breath, that enters your body through your crown, will flow straight through the middle of your brain and touch a small gland called Pineal. That gland, dear one, holds the memory of the beauty of your soul. And not just that. When that gland remembers, every cell of your body remembers. It is so simple. So here, take another breath and see it gently touch your Pineal as it travels to your heart. It's almost like it tickles it, saying, "Hey, wake up, it's time."

"Time for what?" it might ask.

"For this human to remember."

Your breath is not separate from anyone else's breath. If you could see the beauty of the breath of God, a life presence that flows through every single living being, even the rocks of this sacred planet. If you understood that, you would realize you are breathing together with the whole Universe. And that is exciting.

Allow your Pineal to wake up. Allow your body to remember. You are a soul, taking on this body to have an experience. It was meant to be an experience of joy and pure bliss. But it is for you to find out what that means. Breath by breath.

5. Telepathy

"My heart is always open. I explore telepathy and interspecies communication."

Opening the heart is part of many different traditions, and many masters repeatedly take their student's focus back to the center of their chests. And for a good reason. When you open your heart, you start balancing the mind with intuition, feelings and vulnerability. Heart trusts and dreams. Heart knows there's more to life than just survival. There's passion and love. There's courage.

Here's something interesting about dolphins and their pectoral fins: they can't move them around like we can our hands. When I swam with them and experienced telepathy for the first time, I realized pectoral fins represented something very important – dolphins can't close their hearts! They can turn around and swim away, but they can never close their hearts.

So, here is their invitation, can you keep your heart open no matter what happens around you? This truly is the most courageous and most profound level of vulnerability. To show yourself to everyone. To allow your heart to be seen, no matter the circumstances.

Numerology of 5

Number 5 represents change. We're used to opening and closing our hearts, depending on past experiences and how safe we feel in the moment. And now it's time for a change. Put your hands in the position of pectoral fins and feel your heart, as it opens and stays open. This change then allows for a new form of communication, from one open heart to another. Can you imagine a humanity where everybody does this?

Dolphins on Telepathy

And now, it's really time to start expanding. We love it. We know much has been said about your heart and the benefits of living inside your heart. But there's more. Could your heart be an interdimensional connecting point, where many beings and spirits can meet as a guiding force, to help you move forward in a new way?

When you connect two hearts, you build a bridge and suddenly, you know what the other being is feeling and thinking. It's so simple, yet so profound. Do you understand that in this way you can allow anyone to live in your heart? It means that beautiful, sacred, enlightened beings you knew walked this Earth can be in your heart in every moment of every day. We, the dolphins can swim in and out of your heart and remind you of our presence and our gifts whenever you want us to. And not just that. With this presence comes communication. With this presence comes a feeling of connection, that goes deeper that what you would normally feel when you see us. We could call it oneness, but this oneness is all about support, encouragement, and love.

So, your heart is not just yours, it is an Universal heart. It is so big it can literally fit anything and anyone in the Universe who has a heart resonance with you. So, when you bring your soul into your body, through your breath, you can then open your heart and see who has the resonance of your soul. Dear human, you are not alone and never will be, just ask your heart.

We are always with you, if you believe it or not, for we carry the resonance of your soul. You can talk to us whenever you want. All you need to do is open your heart and allow it to find us, and connect with the hearts of the pod, and in will start to pour everything we are and everything we represent. Humans would call this telepathy and inter-species communication, but it's much more than that. It's a family reunion. It's a remembrance of one heart, of the beauty that permeates everything in creation. You are never alone!

6. Multidimensionality

"I am a multidimensional being, filled with light, color and sound. Self-love builds a bridge to my quantum nature. I remember my star origins."

The first time I experienced my multidimensional nature was when I started to "wake up" in my dreams, also known as "Lucid Dreaming." When this happens, you become aware that you are just dreaming, and that realization alone allows you to start changing what's happening around you. Supposedly, anything you wish for can manifest: you can meet with family members who have passed on, you can have a desire to be on the other side of the world and it just happens, you can imagine flying and off you go, ... When a friend of mine shared all that, I thought, "Ok, I need to try it myself." I didn't want to do exercises to get me there (although they can be very helpful), so I just said out loud, "I will experience Lucid Dreaming, whenever the timing is right." I trusted it would happen and it did.

It took half of a year for my first "waking up," and then it would occur every few months. Comparing my experiences to what others shared, I noticed one big difference. When I woke up in my dreams, I had a completely different consciousness! It had no human logic to it and it was in no way connected to the "Jan" part of me, with my usual human thoughts and curiosity. Who was I?

The "I" in my dreams had an enlightened perspective. It had its own logic and its own way of doing things and everything made perfect sense to it. It assisted people with "waking up" in their dreams and also waking up in their lives, by teaching about the New Energy on the planet and how to overcome fear. It was teaching people how to fly and levitate. It was attending sacred mystery schools in halls filled with crystal lights and teachers of high reverence. And most importantly, it knew way way more than my human side could possibly ever know. And all of this was completely natural, almost casual. I concluded it must be my Higher Self or a very enlightened part of me, that was the "I" in my dreams. Something that became clear to me during these dreams is that we are much more than human.

Numerology of 6

Number 6 represents communication, harmony, relationships, and Higher Self. When you connect with the energy of dorsal fin you open the door to a multidimensional communication within your own being, which strengthens your connection to your Higher Self.

Dolphins on Multidimensionality

Here is our favorite point! Why would we have one? Because this one carries within it the seed for understanding everything else. You see, you can't even begin to understand multidimensional reality if you don't first acknowledge that you are more than human. And it is great that your science is trying to explain your origins and discovering you had tails and everything else, but they will never see that your presence, your I AM is not from here. You weren't created on this planet, you helped to create it! You are a timeless, boundless, beautiful being, who really has no beginning and no end. Dorsal fin reminds you that you came from the stars and that there's much more to you than meets the eye. Are you ready to dive in?

Self-love is the basis for self-exploration. The more you remember the love your higher self has for you, the easier you will navigate through the different realities you inhabit. You will start seeing connections where there was none before. You will start enjoying yourself as a spirit more than a human. You will understand that everything in this reality is just a blink of an eye in a grand cosmic scheme of things. Wouldn't that make you laugh? You are endless, and it is time to start shaking off those old beliefs of what it means to be human and start redefining yourself as a more expanded version of yourself. For you see, that's why we're here. We came into our dolphin bodies to show you what happens when you live from a more expanded consciousness.

We promised you, that no matter how deep you go in your human darkness, we would always be there saying, "You came from the stars, you came from the stars." To us it's so easy, because we can't not see it. We look at you and we overflow with joy. "Look at you!" we say. "Look how beautiful and grand and limitless you are." We just love you so much. If we could only tell you how much. But you know. You have that same love inside. We just can't wait to see you again, spirit to spirit and laugh about the days we were playing around on this planet. "It was so much fun." we'll say to each other as we hug and laugh some more. "Let's do it again." Will you remember this time? Will you remember next time? Are you ready to do it right now? You came from the stars! And so it is.

7. Gaia

"I embody Gaia. I am one with the soul of the planet."

Kryon has invited us many times to re-establish a connection with Gaia, as strong as the one that ancients had. That means waking up with gratitude, talking to the planet as a partner and understanding that everything we see around us is part of the abundance this planet has for us. There are cultures from the past and present who live close to the earth, trusting that it will take care of them. Without all the safety nets that are imbedded in modern cultures, they've spent much less time than most modern people worrying about tomorrow. There is a knowing that Gaia provides food, clothing and everything that's needed, every moment of every day. And she does. Are you willing to try it and rediscover that? Can you begin by taking a moment every day, to express your gratitude, your love, and your appreciation for Gaia?

In introduction I described a vision within a vision: a dolphin tail that represented infinite Gaia consciousness focusing into a single point, the body of the dolphin. I now see that the Ancients knew it as well, Gaia lives within us and we are part of her. We are not separate. We are cells in her body and our consciousness is part of her consciousness. It may sound complicated, but you don't need to understand it with your head, all you need to do is feel the love that arises in your heart when you say, "Gaia and I are one."

Numerology of 7

Number 7 stands for divinity, sacredness inside. Can you see the beauty of the system here? Dolphin point 4, that is a Gaia number, represents your soul and Dolphin point 7, that is a divinity number, represents Gaia. Could it be they have to work together for you to get the whole picture? Could it be you have to find divinity under your feet to really understand your soul? Here is a little juicy insight. When you put 4 and 7 together you get an 11, a master number representing spiritual illumination!

Dolphins on Gaia

Dear human, it is time to see the whole picture. It is time to see how this planet is here for you, a playground that responds to your thoughts and actions. Gaia loves you so much and is here in service. Dolphins' tail tells you a secret. Or is it? We are a part of Gaia. Her beauty isn't happy to just be inside rocks, trees and oceans, it wants to live within dolphins as well. Gaia talks through us so you might hear her clearly when you swim with us. She is grand and responsible for everything you see around you. She is your home, for now. She is your environment of support, to really live and express and experience your magnificence.

So, the seventh dolphin point tells you that our secret is now your secret too, "Gaia lives within you as well." This grand being, who is your mother, lives within each cell and breaths with you as you walk around. How is that possible? Welcome to multidimensional reality. You are more than one thing. You are many. It is time to stop defining yourself with your mind, because your mind will never get it. Instead take a deep breath, say I AM, and then celebrate. Why do you think birds sing every day? Multidimensional reality is filled with joy, just celebrating all of existence. This same joy lives within you, the joy of Gaia.

Come back to this planet in a gentle, loving, nurturing way. Come back to her love. Let yourself lie down on a mossy floor in a forest, feeling everything embracing you and knowing you. Let yourself jump into the warm waters of oceans and rivers, releasing everything that you carry. Say out loud, "Gaia lives within me. I am one with the soul of the planet. I know her joy, her growth, her life. I am one with the soul of the planet." Allow yourself to really feel what this means, and allow yourself to join in the choir with the birds, the dolphins, the whales, and every living being. You are precious. Gaia knows you and loves you. And so it is.

• CHAPTER 9 •

The Meaning of 44

"AAAAAHHHH, MY WATER!" I awoke from my sleep by my wife's half excited and half scared cry. I quickly checked the clock and wrote, "7:07am, water broke." into a little spreadsheet that our midwife provided for us. The journey into this world for our daughter Kalalea had begun.

About a month before the due date, I dreamed about her birth. While holding her for the first time, I felt such love that I completely forgot to look at the clock. The dream ended with me frantically trying to figure out what the exact time of her birth was. The next day our doula came for a visit and shared she also had a potent dream that night. She was present at the moment of birth and was asked out loud, "What time is it?" She looked at the clock and it was 3:07. We all thought it was an interesting synchronicity – me asking the question in my dream and her receiving the answer. Fast forward to the moment of Kalalea's arrival one month later, she was born at 3:07am!

The story doesn't end there. My wife's water broke at 7:07am almost two days earlier. It took me a few months to finally do the math and the result made my jaw drop. Not only was Kalalea's time of birth revealed in a dream, it was exactly (to the minute!) 44 hours of labor!

This chapter speaks about the meaning of 44 and how dolphin teachings tie into it. As you will learn shortly, number 44 is a master number, which represents the next step in evolution of humanity. "Wait a minute," some will say, "Humanity is evolving? What does that mean?"

I was first introduced to that idea through Lee Carroll and Jan Tober's book, "The Indigo Children."[1] The main premise of the book was that new kids are becoming more conceptual and carry an increased sense of self-worth. This evolution is not just spiritual and has been noticed by teachers and health care professionals worldwide. Lee Carroll says this process is far from being finished and that we will witness an accelerated shift in the consciousness with every new generation of children.

This is reflected in Tibetan numerology that Kryon speaks about often. I believe numbers are actually carrying encoded information about what happens as humanity evolves. In ancient Tibet they defined the meanings and energies of simple digits from 1-9 and also master numbers 11, 22 and 33. Tibetans never defined the meanings of 44 and higher because human consciousness hasn't yet been ready to receive it.

Kryon has been saying for years, that our DNA efficiency is around 33-35% going towards 44%. Every time he says this, my intuition goes, "Pay attention to the numbers – they are not linear." Meaning, I need to look at the numerology and not linearity of percentage. 33 stands for compassion of the Divine Feminine, 35 makes an 8 which is about manifestation and abundance, but 44 hasn't been defined yet.

Why? Could it be that 44 represents where we're going, but can't be understood until we get there?

I believe master numbers are describing the journey of humanity from lower to higher consciousness. While this journey seems linear, it is not. Next level is not achieved by the amount of time that passes but by our willingness to remember and embody more of our true nature. This is what free choice between light and dark means – we are free, personally and collectively, to choose in any moment to open up to the next level of realization.

My daughter needed exactly 44 hours to be birthed onto this planet. I believe she is telling us she is part of this new wave of consciousness, where the percentage of active DNA gets increased to 44. She was born with all the shifts we've been working on all these years.

Now, let's make the whole story even more exciting. Through Monika Muranyi I found out about research done at Texas A&M University, where they discovered that dolphin DNA has 44 chromosomes. The scientists also stated it is extremely similar to human DNA, more than that of cows, pigs or horses. Are your bells going off right now? 44 chromosomes – this shouts for us to look at the connection here. Could it be that what dolphins carry multidimensionally will help us understand the meaning of 44 and the evolution of humanity?

Letting Go of The Past

As I was diving into this chapter and loving the profundity of the subject, an old "friend" came for a visit, "seed fear". I described it in the fourth chapter, it is the fear of enlightenment, fear of being killed, tortured and persecuted because of one's spiritual knowledge. While it tended to stop me in the past this time it was actually a confirmation: what I was onto was a big deal and is bringing more light onto this planet.

And then, another realization hit me: we can't understand the meaning of 44 unless we clear our Akash of old stuff. We need to reorganize our history to support us fully in claiming this new energy. We can't move forward carrying baggage of fear and low self-worth.

The dolphins channeled a beautiful message about it. I thought it was for me, but then when I read it again, I realized it was for each one of us, ready to step forward.

"Dear human. We are right here with you, look up. You are appreciated and blessed. You are celebrated and embraced, by our energy and our love. Listen: Why do you feel the need to keep being small? How many times have we told you: You carry the God inside. You are beautiful beyond measure. Why do you need to deny this simple truth? You've felt it. Understood it. Realized it. Even claimed it. And then you return to your small you. Why?

We'll tell you: It feels comfortable. It feels like it's you, small you, human you. It's an illusion. And you know it. But you haven't gotten to a place yet where you're willing to let it go. You're still holding onto it, for dear life. Dear one, listen: Your life is eternal. Nothing, absolutely nothing, that happens on this planet can take that away from you. Yes, you've experienced torture in the past, but that is now long gone. Can you repeat that, 'That is now long gone. I am safe and celebrated as I feel the embrace of dolphin love.'

We will walk right beside you as you step into the light. There is no need any more to play the game of being small. You don't benefit. It doesn't serve you or the planet anymore. It is time to embrace your grandness, your beauty, your soul. Do you hear that? It is time and we'll be right beside you, holding your hand. May your light shine again in its original form, not filtered by fears and everything that happened in the past. You are ready. We will stand right beside you as you walk into the light. Dear one, appreciated and loved, you are. Thank you for your courage, thank you for opening up. It is time now, to take the next step as you walk into the light – don't just see the light but become it. Thank you, we love you!"

What Is Real?

Discovering the meaning of 44 was like putting together a puzzle. I often clearly felt something was supposed to be in the book but had no idea in what chapter. One of the key pieces was a message I received from Rebecca Dawson, a channeler, speaker and author, who with the assistance of her "crew": Serapis Bey, St Germain & Kuthumi, disseminates information about the shifts that are occurring for Earth and humanity.[2]

This message was again spoken to me personally, but I knew it was meant to be read and understood by many. It is the first hint pointing us towards 44 and why dolphins are connected to it. Take a deep breath and feel Rebecca's "crew" enter,

"Greetings to you, we are with you, and you are with us in this moment. One moment, one time, one life, one planet... one self. We say to you that fragmentation of human reality has reached its fulcrum. The fragmentation of human reality has meant that humanity in itself is always looking to bring pieces together, is always looking to bring these different fragments of reality back into the one, so that wholeness can occur. For many humans this is what spiritual quest is, 'I want to know more, I want to know God, I want to know the Universe, therefore I must bring the fragmentation back into the one.'

But the knowledge of the beings that you speak of [dolphins and whales], they know in reality that the fragmentation never occurred. Listen carefully, the truth that the ones that live in the ocean hold, is that fragmentation never really occurred!

What if the reality of fragmentation, the reality of 3D perspective, the reality that things are broken, the reality that things have shifted, the reality that there was repair that was necessary... what if that reality is not a reality? What if that reality is a belief? And humans have been sitting among a belief of fragmentation for so long, that all of their focus is on how to solve the problem of it. All of their focus is on, 'What must we do to bring it back into wholeness? We are broken as a people, we are broken as a planet, what must we do?'

What if, all of that is a distraction; what if, all of that is a belief, but not reality? What if, the reality is that this fragmentation never happened? What if, the oceans and those that live in the oceans, your friends, you call them, what if, they hold the truth that the fragmentation never happened? What if, all that is required is a knowing, a remembrance of what is real for it to become real, within the cells, within the body, within human interaction, that fragmentation never occurred?

What if, they are the only ones that hold the truth of that memory on this planet? What if in your interactions with them, your acknowledgment of them, that truth arises in its awareness within your DNA, within your cells and you begin to reverberate the truth that the fragmentation never happened?

Would this not change your view of reality, would this not change your focus? You are no longer interested in repair, or problem-solving or solving the problem of fragmentation on this planet, you are only interested in what is real. And what is real is the wholeness. What is real is the multidimensionality.

So, we say unto you, blessed one, you are here to be the beacon of what is real, the beacon of what is being forgotten, the beacon of what humans believe was lost, but in actuality never was; it's just that humanity became so seduced by an alternative reality that was about fragmentation. We say onto you, you are here to sing the song of remembrance, you are here to sing the song of what is real, because when humanity wakes up to what was never lost, they discover that they were always there in their wholeness."

From Awakening to Merging

The message resonated deeply with my guidance. I had been doing the Inner Dolphin Awakening journey for a while, using the affirmations that I've given you. And then one day my intuition gently nudged me, and I was shown a slight change in affirmations. Instead of using, "I awaken the dolphin within," I was asked to use, "I merge with the dolphin within." My guidance was very clear and specific: it is time to start allowing these two pieces that you call human and dolphin to merge with each other, meaning you stop seeing them as separate. Instead of being one or the other it becomes a dance, co-creation, simply enjoying what arises in the moment. Dolphins shared with me, that when you start merging with one part of your multidimensional self, you begin to remember that you can exist in many places simultaneously, which then opens the door to merging with your higher self – the I AM in everything you are. Here's their perspective,

"Dear human being, welcome to the last step. It might take years or moments to accomplish, but this has always been the last step. You see, you are not separate, the last step is the realization of that. It is the merging with what you now remember as a part of you. It is claiming that which was always yours, becoming it to such a degree, that it becomes part of you and you part of it.

When you merge with your inner dolphin you drop the need to have exercises and affirmations, you simply know you are all that you are. It is inside you, for you have now expanded to a state where you know your consciousness is in many places and you can experience multidimensional reality of self. You become I AM, one and many. Welcome home."

Do you see the similarities in the message here? Rebecca talked about letting go of fragmentation and remembering wholeness. Dolphins urged me to step from awakening to merging – remembering the I AM in every part of my multidimensional nature.

I was asked to change the affirmations first, so I was able to feel what the energy of "merging" meant. I knew there was more to come, and I knew it would be more of an experience and less of a concept, so I wasn't trying to force it – I just kept the doors open. What came next blew my mind.

The Meaning Of 44

It was absolute clarity, delivered through my intuition. The meaning of 44 (and everything beyond that) hasn't been revealed for a reason. It was so obvious, I had no idea how I couldn't see it before. It was once again a "connecting the dots" exercise, that I feel Kryon nudges us to do whenever he channels. It is as if he keeps on saying, "These are the pieces of the puzzle, now put it together!"

Let's first look back at what I talked about in the sixth chapter. I described the multidimensional soul as a flower with many petals that are all expressions of the I AM. I stated that each one of us experienced enlightenment on other planets thus fully merging with the I AM and dropping the limitations of time and space. I asked, "Are you ready yet to take the hand of your star sisters and brothers from different star systems, who all carry the same name in light as you do?"

The love and wisdom that starts pouring in as you take that hand is a gift of self-love, which has the power to melt away human hardship. But there's more. With this connection comes a remembrance, an activation of knowledge that is a part of your Star Akash. This knowledge, dear reader, includes the meaning of 44! You have experienced it before! It is encoded in the time capsules that are on the grids, in your DNA and also in dolphins and whales. Here are Kryon's words,

"The time capsules that are opening, which the Pleiadians have activated, are going to be "seen" by several parts of you. Some, through the grids, but some are seen by the Soul part of you. The Soul part of you is only engageable as you approach 44% (of the efficiency of your DNA). This is the signal for it to fully unfold. Spiritual evolution is going to be an increase in something that we've never talked about, but which you are starting to feel. We're going to call it "Soul remembrance." You are starting to remember things beyond Earth!"[3]

As you start receiving the gifts of the time capsules, your Star Akash reveals the multidimensional nature of your soul. It is an amazing system of empowerment! Dolphins are part of it. Whales are part of it. Releasing the past is part of it. Letting go of fragmentation is part of it. Merging with your multidimensional nature is part of it.

As I looked at all these pieces together there was one final realization. It happened as I sat down with the number 44 and started feeling into its energy. I now ask you to do the same. Join me as we breathe in what 44 represents. It is two 4s standing next to each other, which means they carry a strong Gaia energy, strong energy of the physical and structure. Keep on breathing with that. Two 4s are creating master number 44. The next step in evolution of humanity.

Are you ready to now put all pieces together and look at the bigger picture? (Drum-roll, please.)

The meaning of 44 hasn't been defined yet, because... it can't be! 44 is a personal experience that comes through your body, through your Innate, that can't be described or defined. It has to be experienced!

That's why, dear reader, Inner Dolphin Awakening is about 7 dolphin points on your body, talking to your Innate, opening the time capsules that receive the memory of this experience from the stars. You are bringing the resonance of 44 to you, through your body, through your Innate. Dolphins having 44 chromosomes is a synchronicity, a marker saying, "Become like us and you will get it." And that's why dolphins invite us to just come and play: to get us out of our minds. 44 can't be described or defined – it must be personal, and it will never be a concept for your mind. You need to just get it, or in other words: BECOME IT!

And dear reader, that brings me back to where I started this book.

"Have you ever read a book and when someone asked you what it was about your answer came in one simple sentence? Have you ever wondered why masters just smile instead of saying anything at all?

The experience of inner knowing cannot be replaced by words. It cannot be explained, the only way to grasp it is to take the journey yourself.

This book is not trying to explain the unexplainable. It is an invitation. If there was one sentence, that would describe the whole book it would be, "What if everything you knew to be true about dolphins was inside you?" But maybe it would be better to just smile. Like the masters do. And extend a hand of invitation. Are you ready to take my hand and embark on a journey with me?

SOURCES

1.chapter

[1] Kryon is a loving angelic energy, whose messages are channeled by Lee Carroll, the "original" Kryon channel. Through more than twenty-six years, the loving information from this partnership has sustained many and explained much about our changing times.
Learn more: www.kryon.com
[2] In 1999 Tobias, assisted by Gabriel, Metatron and many others, sent out the clarion call of awakening and reunion. His monthly messages, channeled through his beloved former son, now known as Geoffrey Hoppe, quickly found their way to the hearts of awakening humans, those whom he had worked together with in times long past. With his messages of love, comfort and freedom, Tobias offered unceasing support for humans in what he called "the biggest evolution of consciousness humanity has ever experienced."
Tobias spoke through Geoffrey for ten years, and then chose to return to Earth for a long-awaited lifetime of celebration and joy.
Learn more: www.crimsoncircle.com
[3] Kryon in Salzburg, 2004
http://www.kryon.com/k_chanelhowbig.html

2.chapter

[1] Kryon in Breckenridge, 2001
http://www.kryon.com/k_chanelbreck.html
[2] Kryon in Philadelphia, 2002
http://www.kryon.com/k_chanelphilly.html
[3] Kryon in McCaysville, 2007
http://www.kryon.com/k_chanelhandbook01.html
[4] Muranyi, M.; 2013, The Gaia Effect
https://www.amazon.com/Gaia-Effect-Remarkable-Collaboration-Humanity/dp/289626132X
[5] www.kirael.com
[6] Kryon in Hawaii, 2012
http://www.kryon.com/k_channel12_Hawaii-1.html
[7] Kryon in Hawaii, 2006
http://kryon.com/cartprodimages/downloadcruise7_02.html

4.chapter

[1]https://www.dolphins-world.com/dolphins-in-mythology/
[2] http://www.people-oceans-dolphins.com/index.html
[3] Cressey, J.;.1998, Making a Splash in the Pacific: Dolphin and Whale Myths and Legends of Oceania
[4] Kryon in San Rafael, 2015

http://www.kryon.com/CHAN2015/k_channel15_sanrafael-15.html
[5] www.joanocean.com
[6] http://www.dolphinreef.co.il/experience.aspx
[7] http://www.waterplanetusa.com/dolphin-therapy/
[8] http://www.waterplanetusa.com/harmony-program/

5.chapter

[1] Kryon in Mt. Shasta, 2003
http://www.kryon.com/k_chanelshasta03.html
[2] https://www.pinealtones.com/about/
[3] http://www.lemurianchoir.com
[4] http://thepathlighter.com
[5] Kryon in Hawaii, 2012
http://www.kryon.com/cartprodimages/download_L-Choir-channels_12.html
[6] Kryon in New Zealand, 2010
http://www.kryon.com/cartprodimages/download_Auckland_1_10.html
[7]http://monikamuranyi.com/extras/gaia-effect-extras/nodes-and-nulls/
[8] http://www.lemurianconnection.com
[9] Kryon in Arkansas, 2016
http://www.kryon.com/cartprodimages/2016%20downloads/download_C-Choir_16.html

6.chapter

[1] Kryon in Mt. Shasta 2013
http://www.kryon.com/cartprodimages/2013%20downl
oads/download_Shasta-Disc-Fri_13.html
[2] Muranyi, M.; 2015, The Human Soul Revealed
http://www.kryon.com/k_71.html
[3] Kryon in Tuscon, 2014
http://www.kryon.com/CHAN2014/k_channel14_TUCS
ON.html
[4] Kryon in San Rafael, 2015
http://www.kryon.com/CHAN2015/k_channel15_sanraf
ael-15.html
http://monikamuranyi.com/extras/gaia-effect-
extras/nodes-and-nulls/
[5] Kryon in Mt. Shasta, 2013
http://www.kryon.com/cartprodimages/2013%20downl
oads/download_Shasta-Disc-Fri_13.html
[6] Kryon in McCaysville, 2007
http://www.kryon.com/k_chanelhandbook01.html
[7] https://youtu.be/uhClBGZj9vQ
[8] http://www.thestargateexperienceacademy.com
[9] Recorded at the Stargate Summer Camp, Mt. Shasta, 2017, http://www.thestargateexperienceacademy.com
[10] https://www.youtube.com/watch?v=ARvZK5rgKyo

7.chapter

[1] Kryon in Portland, 2015
http://www.kryon.com/CHAN2015/k_channel15_portland-15.html

8.chapter

[1] Kryon in Mt.Shasta, 2014
http://www.kryon.com/cartprodimages/2014%20downloads/download_Shasta_14.html Sunday Channel
[2] Carroll, L.; 2017, The New Human. Pg.81
[3] I use Tibetan numerology as taught by Kryon/Lee Carroll/Barbara Dillinger. There's a perfect description on Monika Muranyi's webpage.
http://monikamuranyi.com/articles/energy-numbers/
[4] http://www.compassionatebreath.net

9.chapter

[1]https://www.amazon.com/Indigo-Children-Kids-Have-Arrived/dp/1561706086
[2] https://www.rebeccadawson.net
[3] Kryon in San Rafael, 2015
http://www.kryon.com/CHAN2015/k_channel15_sanrafael-15.html

Made in the USA
Lexington, KY
03 October 2018